I0048792

# ABLE VISIONARY
# LEADERS
## VOL. 1

# ABE
PUBLISHING PRESS

**ABE**
PUBLISHING PRESS

Copyright © ABLE Publishing Press
First published in Australia in 2023
by ABLE ABLE Publishing Press

All rights reserved. No part of this book may be used or reproduced by any means, graphic, electronic, or mechanical, including photocopying, recording, taping or by any information storage retrieval system without the written permission of the copyright owner except in the case of brief quotations embodied in critical articles and reviews.

Because of the dynamic nature of the Internet, any web addresses or links contained in this book may have changed since publication and may no longer be vaild. The views expressed in this work are solely those of the author and do not necessarily reflect the views of the publisher and the publisher hereby disclaims any responsibility for them.

NATIONAL
LIBRARY
OF AUSTRALIA

A catalogue record for this
work is available from the
National Library of Australia

National Library of Australia Catalogue-in-Publication data:
ABLE Visionary Leadership Vol. 1/ ABLE Publishing Press

ISBN: 978-0-6454663-9-3
(Paperback)

# CONTENTS

# INTRODUCTION
# PIONEERING THE PATH TO
# TRANSFORMATIONAL LEADERSHIP

IN THE EVER-EVOLVING TAPESTRY of human history, certain individuals stand as beacons of inspiration, guiding us through the labyrinth of challenges and opportunities. These individuals are not merely leaders; they are visionaries, architects of tomorrow's world. Their stories are etched into the annals of time, their influence shaping the destinies of nations, businesses, and communities. They are the heart and soul of our anthology, *ABLE Visionary Leaders: The passion of a visionary leader.*

In this anthology, we embark on a journey through the stories of leadership, guided by the wisdom and experiences of twenty extraordinary individuals. These authors, hailing from diverse backgrounds, represent a mosaic of perspectives – business leaders who have charted unprecedented success, have fostered social change, and who have navigated the complexities of governance with commitment and dedication. Each author shares their unique vision of leadership, offering profound insights into the challenges they have faced, the lessons they have learned, and the dreams that continue to fuel their journeys.

The theme of this anthology, 'the vision of visionary leader', is a testament to the power of foresight and the belief in a brighter future. These visionary leaders, through their relentless pursuit of their visions, have transformed industries, uplifted communities and left indelible imprints on the world. Their stories serve as a clarion call to aspiring leaders, urging them to envision the change they wish to see and to muster the courage to manifest that change.

As we delve into the pages of *ABLE Visionary Leaders,* we are confronted with a multitude of leadership styles, philosophies and ideologies, each as unique as the individuals who pen these narratives. Yet, at the heart of every story, there exists a common thread – a vision that transcends self-interest, a commitment to making the world a better place, and an unwavering determination to overcome adversity.

Let's embark on a brief exploration of the core tenets that define visionary leadership. We will endeavor to grasp the essence of what it means to be a visionary leader, the qualities that set them apart, and the transformative power of their visions.

## VISIONARY LEADERSHIP: A GLIMPSE INTO THE ESSENCE

Visionary leadership is not a solitary trait or a one-size-fits-all approach. Rather, it is a dynamic interplay of values, beliefs and actions that inspire and mobilize individuals and organizations toward a common goal. A visionary leader is an architect of dreams, a catalyst for change and a steadfast guardian of the vision they hold.

At the heart of every visionary leader's journey lies a profound vision – a vivid mental image of a future that is better than the present. This vision is more than a mere daydream; it is a magnetic force that pulls them and those around them forward, propelling them toward a destiny yet to be realized. The vision serves as a North Star, a guiding light that illuminates the path through turbulent seas and dark nights.

But what distinguishes visionary leaders from the rest? It is their ability to translate their vision into reality, to bridge the gap between aspiration and actualization. This translation requires not only a clear vision but also the tenacity to overcome obstacles, the capacity to inspire others, and the humility to learn from failures.

Visionary leaders are, by nature, disruptors. They challenge the status quo and question conventional wisdom. They are unafraid to take calculated risks and to chart uncharted territories. Their actions often defy the boundaries of what is considered possible, and in doing so, they redefine the realm of possibility for those who follow in their wake.

The authors featured in this anthology each embody a unique set of qualities that characterize visionary leadership. While the specifics may vary, some common traits emerge as we examine their narratives.

**Clarity of Vision:** A leader's vision is not clouded by ambiguity. It is crystal clear and unwavering. It serves as a guiding force, helping them make decisions, set priorities and rally others to their cause.

**Passion and Purpose:** Visionary leaders are driven by an unrelenting passion for their vision. They believe in their purpose with such intensity that it becomes infectious, igniting the hearts and minds of those around them.

**Resilience:** The path of a visionary leader is fraught with challenges. They face adversity head-on, bounce back from setbacks and remain undeterred in the face of criticism or failure.

**Courage:** Courage is the bedrock of visionary leadership. These leaders confront fear and uncertainty, daring to tread where others hesitate. Their courage inspires others to step out of their comfort zones.

**Innovation:** Visionary leaders are innovators by nature. They constantly seek new solutions, challenge existing paradigms and are unafraid to embrace change.

**Empathy and Inclusivity:** They possess the ability to empathize with others' perspectives and experiences. They build bridges, fostering inclusivity and diversity in their organizations and communities.

**Effective Communication:** Visionary leaders are compelling communicators. They can articulate their vision in a way that resonates with others, inspiring collaboration and action.

**Long-Term Thinking:** They possess the ability to think beyond short-term gains. Their vision extends into the distant future, guiding their decisions with a focus on sustainable, enduring impact.

**Adaptability:** In a rapidly changing world, adaptability is paramount. Visionary leaders are flexible, able to adjust their strategies while remaining true to their core vision.

**Servant Leadership:** They understand that leadership is not about wielding power but about serving others. They lead by example, putting the needs of their teams and communities first.

These qualities, interwoven with the diverse experiences and backgrounds of our authors, paint a comprehensive picture of visionary leadership – one that is both inspiring and attainable for those who seek to follow in their footsteps.

## THE POWER OF STORIES: A BEACON FOR ASPIRING LEADERS

The stories within this anthology are not just biographical accounts; they are roadmaps for those who aspire to become visionary leaders in their own right. They offer valuable insights, lessons and wisdom gained through years of dedicated effort and unwavering commitment.

As you turn the pages of this anthology, you will encounter the narratives of business leaders who transformed fledgling start-ups into global giants. You will witness the journeys of community leaders who galvanized neighbourhoods to create positive change from the ground up. And you will gain insights from government leaders who navigated the complex web of bureaucracy to enact meaningful reforms.

These stories are not limited to the successes alone; they also delve into the struggles, setbacks and moments of doubt that are an integral part of every visionary leader's path. They serve as a reminder that even the most exceptional leaders faced adversity and encountered roadblocks, but it was their resilience and unwavering commitment to their vision that propelled them forward.

It is our hope that these stories will inspire you to embark on your own journey of leadership, armed with the knowledge that visionary leadership is not reserved for a select few. It is a calling that can be answered by anyone with the courage to dream, the determination to act and the willingness to learn from both successes and failures.

## CONCLUSION: A JOURNEY BEGINS

As we embark on this journey through the lives and visions of the twenty remarkable individuals featured in *ABLE Visionary Leaders* let us remember that leadership is not a destination but a continuous journey of growth and self-discovery. The stories within these pages are not just tales of triumph but also a testament to the enduring power of human potential.

May these narratives serve as a source of inspiration, guidance and encouragement to all those who seek to make a positive impact on the world. Whether you are a seasoned leader seeking to refine your vision or an aspiring leader taking your first steps, may this anthology remind you that the vision of a visionary leader can shape the course of history, and that vision resides within each and every one of us.

Together, let us explore the depths of visionary leadership, for it is through our collective commitment to visionary ideals that we can illuminate a path toward a brighter and more promising future for all.

Welcome to *ABLE Visionary Leaders*. The journey begins here.

# CATHERINE MOLLOY
## SEEING WITH THE MIND'S EYE

*Never let yesterday use up today.*

THE LATIN ROOT OF *vis* is to see. The Latin root of *ion* means action or condition.

Vision – it's an action to see with the mind's eye.

The meaning of *ary* is belonging to/connected.

Visionary leader – is connecting/belonging to the vision seen.

## FUTURE THOUGHTS

Have you ever had a future thought or seen the future and if you took action and moved in a certain direction … it came true?

## A BIG VISION

The last big vision I saw was in 2018. We owned a large house in Buderim and my husband and I had been living there for thirty years. As I work in many cities around the world, and with many people, I felt when I came home, I just wanted to reconnect with the earth and be peaceful. I drew a house I wanted to build and thought I'd like some land so if anything happened in the world there would be a place for our family where we could grow vegetables, fruit, raise animals and be self-sufficient if we had to. Why did I think this? As my husband was semiretired, I thought the country is a great place to rebuild strength and enjoy the outdoors. I also thought there might be enough space to run retreats and we could have some Airbnbs if we ever needed to supplement our income in our retirement years. We quite like having guests and sharing nights under the stars, fires and stories. We were paying a mortgage still and I thought why … why don't we invest this money in a property that pays for itself? So, within a month a property came into my emails, even though I hadn't started looking yet and we haven't moved in thirty years. It had four buildings on it … four homes. We have three children and ourselves … four dwellings if we ever needed them – amazing, right! As we drove onto the seventeen-acre property my husband looked over at me and thought okay, so this is it.

Apparently, I was beaming. But how can we possibly buy a property to live on when we have only looked at one in thirty years? We stopped the car and started to walk on the property; I walked past a very old mango tree with many beautiful succulents growing up the trunk, and as I turned around to look back, I saw a vision of children laughing and running around. Wow, this property had a great feeling and after all, I was hoping for some grandchildren in five years' time. Definitely room for a pony, a ten-by-five pool and a tennis court to boot. And there was a forty-year-old split-level house with wooden floors, and when we walked to the side of the house here was the drawing that I had created a month earlier on how the house should look if we built it! How and why did this happen so easily?

I believe part of being a visionary leader is being open to move in the direction of your dream, visions, thoughts or what you've been shown. It isn't always easy for some, but it is worth it. The old saying 'follow your dreams' is really taking action on what your mind's eye is seeing. Not what your head is trying to protect you from: failure. Believing and trusting is a very difficult condition for human beings to step into.

One of my top strengths is strategy – the ability to lead ourselves, our teams and our organisations in a way that advances the organisation's missions and goals and creates advantage for the long-term. In this definition, there's alignment between our goals and our actions. This is different to dreams and visions. However, once I see the vision I can go to strategy, and I can see the end result and how and what we need to do to get there.

I had no idea that the world would shut down in 2020. However, I saw a place that my family could be together if we ever needed it, and of course eighteen months later that is exactly what the farm was used for – family, then Airbnbs when we were allowed to open up after COVID-19, and now retreats for leaders and speakers and authors.

I hope you can now see how a thought of what the future could be – perhaps a passing dream seen by the mind's eye – is actually a vision you can turn into reality. Where do these visions come from? For me, I would say spirit, and I believe in God which for me really helps with purpose and wanting to help others. I can only guide you through what I know, have seen and experienced. We all have our own thoughts that we do need to be careful of because what we think isn't always true, what we see and vision can be. If it is a kind, loving and a thought not to hurt anyone else then you know it's from a good place, and maybe, just maybe, you should follow it. Ever thought of someone and then they ring, or you bump into them? *Hmmmm.* When I think of someone now, I always reach out and send a thoughtful message and the responses are always quite incredible! Try it next time you think of someone and just maybe it is the start of the visions to share the care factor.

## ANOTHER BIG VISION

In 2009, my husband fell ill and stopped work, never to return, we nearly lost everything in the GFC. The vision that came to me was building a training company – everyone needs customer service, right? … And I love sharing learnings … well, they might need service for their business but they wanted leadership and management so that was no problem because to lead is to serve as well!

My vision was to grow the business. I hate seeing businesses suffer and close usually due to the way we think, our actions, the way we treat others, ourselves, staff and customers. You see, every business is in the service business, or you would have no customers. I wanted to recoup our millions of lost dollars and through this process support others in need through fundraising and giving from our profits. Something bigger and greater than me to keep going, to grow our business and others at the same time. To create a purpose bigger than just replacing what we lost. Chapter three in my book *The Conscious Leader* is called 'Lead with Purpose' all around purpose-driven leadership.

Aligning values and work to drive purpose and a great reason for living. It also adds the fun factor to work when you are helping others achieve their goals too. Helping feed and clothe the world or even just one person makes a difference.

## WHAT DO YOU SEE IN A CRISIS

In a moment of utter crisis, I saw exactly what I needed to do, and when we are on track it's worth taking a moment to notice how you feel. So you can seek out this feeling again and again. Our emotions create motion – good or bad, so seek the good.

I love to reflect to see if we are living on purpose, aligning to what we are good at and even remembering the visions we had as a child and what made our hearts sing … are you doing any of those things today?

## WHAT DID YOU LOVE AS A CHILD

I was orphaned and adopted between two to three months old from the children's hospital in Brisbane. Funnily enough, as a child I looked after the stray animals and stuck up for anyone being bullied at school and for those that didn't fit in, I always did my best to be inclusive. I fundraised for the children's hospital in Brisbane from grade five and even to this day take up storybooks for the children in hospital over Christmas. I love stories; they can take you to places you've never imagined or ever been! Today, I still fundraise and have worked with orphans in Uganda since 2009. I believe we can make a difference through education and my vision is in three generations time the work we are doing today will have paid off in the minds of the people there today. We must think differently to get different results. Did you know that Indigenous Australians look seven generations ahead (that's 140-150 years) – they are conscious of what they are doing in the present to make it better for the future. I always say your presence in the present matters.

I lost my mum at sixteen, and today I speak to motherless daughters – the girls with wings.

As a child I loved horses, my third word after mum and dad was horse, and today, I own and ride my own horses.

Being with horses there is a sense of freedom, fun, adventure, love, risk and to lead well we need to slow our heart rate and breathe so the horse is also relaxed in our presence, something we also need to do to lead others well.

I had a farm as a young girl and now live on a farm with goats, rescue sheep, chickens, dogs and horses – this was my dream as a young child.

## WHAT IS YOUR VISION

What did you dream of as a child? Are you living your dream life? By doing this as a visionary leader we are creating and leaving legacies. We can show others the way.

Your visions help shape your legacies, your legacies are your life; the why you are here on the planet not what we can take but what can we give. My visons don't necessarily come to me through meditation; I'm the worst meditator … sixteen seconds (my next book, by the way) is it for me and the thought or vision has arrived, and I do love walking meditations and even talking meditations. As a keynote speaker travelling the world and speaking, words are important to me and what I speak out sometimes is even a surprise for me! Thoughts come in and sow some seeds. It's not about speaking just any thought that pops into our head, you see, the quality of our words determine the quality of our lives and the lives of those around us. So, remember to speak quality words that don't just fuel the fires but help put them out, help share the solutions.

## MY LEADERSHIP JOURNEY

It has always been a conscious one. What am I doing today that will make a difference tomorrow and that will be a good impact for the next generation? How can what I do today make a difference now in people's lives for the better, for them to want to share this with others too?

A positive quote on socials, sending a message to someone in need, working on the next project, keeping money coming in to support family and the people in need that we work with. Thinking smarter to make a difference. Social media has changed the playing field, and we can reach more people today which means we can have a bigger impact even faster. So be conscious of what you are putting out there.

Understanding my values (completing these exercises in my book *The Conscious Leader*) and aligning my purpose with these has been what stood me in good stead when we started our life over again in our forties. When I started my training company Auspac Business Advantage, I realised the need to help others and give back. It started at 10% of profits to local organisations and as I started travelling as a speaker and facilitator, I found the need to help the poorest of the poor get the basics right. Food, water, shelter, clothing, education. When I was asked to write a book as I was speaking on *The Million Dollar Handshake* I didn't want to, then I thought if I align it to our charity Watoto we could give a third of the profits to the orphans with the hope we might sell a million books one day!

## WHAT IS YOUR LEGACY

Starting my business that went international and working with many people to build their businesses, strengthen their teams, build their confidence and help them to communicate at a higher level is part of the legacy I am leaving. You see, no matter where I work in the world, the one thing I have discovered is communication is the number-one most-needed skill in any business. The way you communicate to self, others and understanding the context of communication, being a conscious emotionally intelligent leader (CEIL) is important.

I am creating new CEILs worldwide as part of my legacy helping people break the glass ceiling in leadership and truly understand their domino effect in conversations and actions. This is my mission on this planet. Understanding the human condition through body, mind and spirit. Take a moment to reflect on your micro and/or macro legacies – what are you passing on to the next generation to make a difference to people, animals and planet?

## CLOSING THOUGHTS

The world doesn't need more thought leaders; I believe the world needs more thought*ful* leaders. The visionary leaders of the future will be present today. They will see what we need to make a difference and understand how it may affect future generations by the actions we take today or by the actions we choose not to take today. Sometimes not taking action can be just as damaging as taking the wrong action!

WHAT IF THE FUTURE OF THE WORLD WAS A REFLECTION OF YOU? … the future … is YOU.

What is your mind's eye seeing? Create a vision for your legacy – your legacy is your life. Your life is your story, and your story lives on in those that love you … visualise a life worth leading.

# ABOUT CATHERINE

INTERNATIONAL SPEAKER, AUTHOR AND mother to three children, five horses, four sheep, three goats, eight hens, two dogs and wife to only one husband has been published by Hachette Australia & New Zealand with the international rights sold to Orion Books UK (Harry Potter Fame). They made her first book *The Million Dollar Handshake* business book of the year in 2018 for 7 Dials UK.

This book went on to be an international bestseller and was released in twelve commonwealth countries, and throughout airports and bookshops around the world. ACME publishing house bought the rights to release it in Taiwanese for the Taiwan, Hong Kong and Macau markets and by First News in Vietnam and released in Vietnamese.

*The Conscious Leader* was Catherine's second book released through covid for this decade of emerging leaders. It is award winning and an amazon bestseller.

Catherine is fun, friendly and forward thinking; she has spoken on stages from Saudi Arabia through to India, China and over 120 cities worldwide. Soon to speak in her first castle in Ireland with KMD Books Australia. As a communication expert Catherine Molloy reveals the hidden psychology behind connection and influence and provides people with the keys to revolutionise their communication effectiveness.

She has featured in many magazines worldwide from *LA Weekly* to *Belfast Times*. She has appeared on Australian and Indian TV and has written and been featured in eight other books world wide.

Catherine was made a global goodwill ambassador for her humanitarian work in 2017 and travels to Uganda to help build homes for orphans and vulnerable children, she has worked closely with Watoto since 2009 and she loves all the people of the world, yes you too!

# KAREN McDERMOTT
## INSPIRED LEADERSHIP

*Once we align our values with our ambitions then we can make any-thing happen because by harnessing the super fuel of loving perspective, anything is possible. Because LOVE is the super fuel of all success.*

BEING A VISIONARY LEADER is a whole new way of leading. I like to call it inspired leadership. It is where we walk our talk, and we show instead of telling. Gone are the outdated leaders of the past who dictate, who are all about saying how they want it to be done. Inspired leadership is about being innovative, thinking outside of the box, thinking new pro-gressional thoughts and for me, I do that personally through my seven master gifts that I live through and have written books on, and speak about all the time. I have had huge successes in my life, and also my share of fails. But I don't dwell on failures because failures are kind of challenges. Challenges are going to come in every quest because that is where the growth is. If you are someone like me who sets big goals and pursues big things, there's going to be lots of challenges because there's lots of growth that needs to happen for things to happen. The bigger the thing you want to happen, the more you're going to have to grow into it so that the very next natural step is to receive your goal. This is why self-development journeys always come with challenges. It is advanta-geous to have a renewed perspective of challenges, that challenges are growth opportunities!

There are always struggles before a breakthrough, but that doesn't mean the journey to receiving what it is you want to achieve has to be unfulfilling. There's nothing more fulfilling than the journey. I always find the quest, the challenges, the growth that happens, the person you become. We all live through cycles, and I go on journeys to make something happen and then I'll move on.

They require you to be very much wider in your thinking and higher in your vibration and you have to be very mindful and steadfast in that approach. It's about being aware, also being mindful and thinking, making an effort for the conscious decisions that you're making and how others are reacting to that and how you're reacting to that. So really being mindful of and being aware. It's likened the awakening where you see things wider and deeper and also you react from a higher vibration so that you don't take things personally, you see things for what they are and have empathy and understanding around others.

My master gifts as an inspired leader are mindfulness, knowing, intention, love, gratitude, forgiveness and belief.

## MINDFULNESS

Mindfulness in leadership is very important, because mindfulness is the essence of magic, it's the essence of not having those boundaries that others do. If you're mindful of your behaviour and other people's behaviour, you will also be able to make huge things happen in your life. Mindfulness is one of the keys and that's why it's one of my first principles, really not ignoring your intuition, really allowing your intuition to guide you. Because within you, that knowing that we're all born with within you is the power to make decisions with unwavering confidence.

It means that you can say yes or no in a split second so that you never miss out on an opportunity that's aligned with where you're going. And you also have the courage to say no to an opportunity that's not aligned with where you're going. You can do that with love.

Being aware of your thoughts is the first major step towards creating a life you will love. Our thoughts create our reality. They are responsible for the energy we emit. They are responsible for what we put out into the world and how others perceive us. They are all powerful. So it makes sense that we should be in control of them, right? Mindfulness is the most natural way to control your thoughts. Being aware of what is happening around you is common sense! Then why do more of us not embrace it? Does it go against our human nature? Have we grown so far away from a mindful mindset that it takes a total conscious mind shift to help us find the perfect flow? I am fascinated by how our minds work and especially how powerful they are. Our perceptions of life and the things that go on around us are often not aligned with where we want to be in life and so often you can feel unsettled, as if everything is against you or you just don't feel fulfilled.

There are no limits, only those we impose on ourselves. We are all different and we all think differently! This is fabulous as can you imagine how bland the world would be if we were all the same? Variety is the spice of life! However, there is this universal law that is supported on a metaphysical level.

## KNOWING

I use one strategy in manifesting everything in my life – the Knowing strategy. When I don't use this strategy I make mistakes and experience unnecessary and often costly detours when working towards achieving my dreams and goals. Destiny is there for us all to embrace but many of us settle with playing safe or get so distracted by the dazzling attraction of external objects that we waste time in reaching our highest potential. It is when we reach our highest potential that the race for success ends and a new more relaxed pace of life is there for us to embrace if that is what we choose. There is profound comfort in the Knowing that you have succeeded in manifesting a deep-rooted desire, that all of your hard work and risk-taking has paid off. It is from this position that the world is your oyster and you can stand confident in the Knowing that you have made magic happen and can do it again if you so choose.

We have the power to control our feelings so we can manipulate our destiny and attract any number of desires. I have used this successfully on many occasions. So how is Knowing different? Knowing is your internal compass, a skill you were born with and can access anytime. It's true power in the alignment with your true purpose and highest potential.

## INTENTION

It can be hard to believe in something if you can't see it with your eyes or feel it with your hands. Yet the most amazing things that have happened in my life have come from having faith that all will turn out exactly as it is meant to, and that I will show up and go on the journey when needed to move things along. I one hundred percent believe in the magic of intention. There is science in it but I love to think of the magic in it too. One thing we do not want to do is feed into the cycle of overthinking as that often leads to analysis paralysis and that serves no one. Had I overthought when I set the intention to write my first novel in 2010 it would not have happened and had that not happened, I would not have found my true calling and path into publishing. It does not bear thinking about! But the seed was planted when a conversation I had with a friend gifted me the belief that writing a novel was possible. I had limiting beliefs around that, which I had to shatter. When I started to believe in the possibility, I also became more open minded and aware of the signs coming my way that led to writing my first book. Once that limiting belief was dispelled there was nothing holding me back. No excuses could be made, possibility grew into potential and subsequently a series of serendipitous events led to me sitting down to write my first book which was the biggest catalyst in my life.

Had I not set that one intention I would never have joined the dots together to where I stand today. Set intentions and believe in them with all of your heart! Be brave!

## LOVE

Understanding that love is the purest form of energy and a power that we all have the instant ability to access can be a bit overwhelming for some people. I've talked many times about it being an infinite well that we can access at any time, and it is! We often get hurt in life and shield ourselves from love when in fact it is in those moments that we need to bask more in it. Some people unconsciously lock it away because of fear due to the things that have happened in their past and their vulnerability when they open up their hearts and share love.

To connect to love you will need to find stillness. In this busy bee world we now live in, it can be tough to access love straight away. If you do not already have an automatic tendency to go to love when acting or reacting then you will need to rewire your heart and mind.

Loving energy is the super fuel of success, when you pursue something with loving intention it will not only happen faster it will also happen in the best possible way. Highest potential success and the highest potential personal growth.

## GRATITUDE

You can't lose when you tap into this high frequency energetic vibration. Gratitude alone will get results but if you want to experience next level experiences you will first be in the energy of gratitude and allow the essence of the emotions you are feeling to ripple through you so that you are emitting a high energy frequency. It is at this point when you should navigate some energy into what you want to manifest in your future. Then when inspired thoughts and/or opportunities aligned with those intentions present themselves to you, you will know. If you have the courage to action them straight away you will achieve results higher than you can ever imagine.

Being grateful is a wonderful virtue and also an amazing tool for positioning yourself where you want to be in the future. You need to be grateful now for whatever you wish to experience in your life in order to have it in your future. It is a beautiful cycle that when you allow it to flow will create bucket loads of magic in your life. One of the best ways to regulate high vibrational gratitude emotions is to prioritise joy as much as possible.

## FORGIVENESS

You might not think forgiveness and money would go hand in hand, however it is important to consider them in relation to each other. Money is energy according to the universal laws and any blocks you have around it are because of your energy around it. Therefore, it's important that you embrace forgiveness when it comes to money. That can be forgiveness in the sense of your own financial habits and spending, or it can be forgiveness for how you earn or receive money from others.

There has to be forgiveness around every aspect of money. Your energy around it needs to be clear from guilt, shame, any sense of being unworthy, or feeling like a charity case. What I always suggest is that you forgive yourself all of that, along with any limiting beliefs from childhood. Many people hold onto shame that is not theirs and not understanding how the universal laws work, they live in poverty. Release yourself from that energy and gravitate instead into gratitude. There is abundance in gratitude. When we're grateful for what we have, we will have more to be grateful for. Our world needs more good people earning good money so that more good things will happen on this planet. Let me repeat that: We need more good people earning good money so that good things can happen in the work we do. Faith and forgiveness are imperative when it comes to money. Our mindset sets the scene, it's the launch pad and the landing pad, that's why forgiveness is important. Forgive yourself and others if you have money blocks. Love what you have, live for what you love, and really enjoy the life that you have with confidence, knowing that you are deserving of it all. Money that comes from bad energy will only bring unpleasant results. It's important to be true to your values when it comes to calling in money. If you hold any shame or guilt around it, go into forgiveness. Release the shame and guilt and move into gratitude as quickly as you can.

## BELIEF

When others believe in us and when we believe in others, it brings out the magic within someone. Sometimes people don't know their own gifts and we are given the insight into what their gift is. They may not see it for themselves until we voice it or share it. Quite often it comes through a compliment, an observation, or maybe intuitively. Some things just come to us, we share it with them and it ignites something within them. It may not be in that moment when we say it to them, but our words, our belief, and maybe our actions that follow through for them can spark something in their life that they may not have thought about pursuing. It can be a big catalyst in their life. I speak from experience here, and also from observing other people's success journeys. Quite often, someone will make a comment without any idea it will have a profound impact on the other person's life in that moment.

Belief, paired with loving intention, makes beautiful things happen in our world, for us and for others, so it has a ripple effect.

Inspired leaders believe in themselves but also see the gifts in others. In turn, someone can borrow the inspired leader's belief until their belief in themselves kicks in. This is a beautiful process when embraced.

It is my hope that my master gifts help future inspired leaders to awaken to their potential and realise the gifts that they have to share with the world. Leadership doesn't have to be loud, but there must be courage and action and a desire to help others.

Being an inspired leader is not the easiest of choices, but it is the most fulfilling as it helps people find the best of themselves and in turn that has a ripple effect that will be felt for generations.

# ABOUT KAREN

KAREN MCDERMOTT IS THE founder of Duchess Serenity Press, a division of Serenity Press that showcases the books she works alongside Sarah Ferguson, Duchess of York, to create. A woman who believes in the power of storytelling to help people achieve their highest potential. Karen's vision is to create platforms that enable people to share their stories and tap into the magic and infinite possibilities within themselves. She is a successful author of novels, non-fiction, children's and life-enhancing journals. She founded Serenity Press, a traditional publishing press that has made waves in Australia, winning many prestigious awards.

Karen's unique ability to strategically leverage business and magic to help her clients achieve their highest potential sets her apart. Her energy is endearing and draws people to her, and she believes in seeing the best in everyone and helping them see the best in themselves.

A passion for inspiring others led Karen to establish the Making Magic Happen Academy, where she hopes to inspire others to pursue their heart-centred passions and live their true life purpose. She believes that everyone has a story to share and that writing has the power to heal.

Through gratitude and the law of loving intention, Karen has created and lived her dream life to the fullest.

Karen is a publisher/founder at Duchess Serenity Press, KMD Books, Serenity Press, Everything Publishing Academy and MMH Press.

# ROBYN BAKER
# LEAVING A LASTING LEGACY FOOTPRINT

*I believe that our impact is our legacy and the only real footprint we leave behind in this world.*

I DON'T BELIEVE THAT we start out with a vision to be a leader – well at least I didn't. My vision was to be a great role model for the team I was working with at the ripe old age of twenty-two where I had to lead a team who, most, were all older than me, and whilst they all had life experience on their side, I had the work-based experience on mine as I had started my working career young and then decided to study as a mature-age student whilst working – what was I thinking!

My managers at the time had indicated to me that they believed me to be an emerging leader, and I personally found this daunting – me, a leader?! (Yep, self-imposter syndrome kicked in hard.) I didn't find out until much later that they had written on my file that I had entrepreneurial skills and showed a rare ability to connect disconnected and disengaged teams. They saw in me what I didn't see in myself, and with their encouragement, this was the beginning of my journey.

Continuing from this first leadership role, I went on to lead many more where I discovered my passion was not in my day-to-day role but in the roles that took me outside of this for a set period of time to evaluate and assess applications. I became interested in what others were doing to make a difference in the world and how myself working in a government role was pivotal to their continuance in serving their communities. How something I considered so small within my role was so important to them and how my decisions were making a difference also. This became something that lit a fire within me, something that drove me to discuss with my team at the time that what we were doing wasn't just a job, it was changing people's lives and no matter how small those decisions seemed they were important to someone.

I'm a great believer that if you are passionate about what you do, you'll never work another day in your life. Your passion will drive you – not only will you love your work but inspire others to love what they do.

I see a great leader as one who is a great role model and inspires others. I am very proud to look back now to many instances that I can say – at the time I didn't realise – but helped shape those who I lead to become great leaders themselves. I can also say that I have stayed in touch with many of those I worked with throughout my career who at the time saw me as their superior and I considered them as a crucial member of our team. I never really regarded myself as their 'boss' or superior, but I always believed that we were a team and without all of us passionately working towards a successful goal then everything would come to a standstill.

I can recall one incidence in particular, and I know the team member recalls it too as we have discussed it over the years a number of times, where a member of my team was upset by something that had happened and the way in which they were spoken to by another who considered themselves everyone's superior, which they weren't, and regardless they didn't have any right to speak to anyone in the manner to which they did. My team member was so upset to the point of crying and threatening to quit. Her emotions were at a high and the person who had said the upsetting comments was oblivious. My priority was to calm my team member down to rational thinking and diffuse the situation. This was accomplished by talking about the conversation, validating her feelings (as they were very valid and real) and discussing what came next. Part of the next step was to take the offender aside and discuss with them the ramifications of treating someone junior in this manner and the words they used not being appropriate or effective for the outcome that they were looking for. Keeping the team working efficiently, whilst it should have been my priority wasn't initially as I felt it was more important to be compassionate than functional. This proved to be the best decision as inevitably the entire team did continue to be productive whilst gaining sympathetic knowledge of what each other needed to be valued within the team along with how to speak to each other in a considerate manner. I am very proud to say that the team continued working well together long after I left to work in another area and the member who wished to quit stayed on and has since become a considerate, sympathetic, visionary leader in a senior executive position within a large organisation with over ten thousand employees. I am also proud to call her my friend after knowing each other for over thirty years – how many leaders can say that?!

When I recall my most significant achievements as a leader, I think of this occasion along with many others where guiding and building up others to be their best selves was important and I think of them fondly as being a part in their development as leaders in their chosen fields. Many I have stayed friends with. Some still call on me to discuss challenges they have within their teams and ask what I would do – I love that they value my opinion. I believe the greatest gift we can give anyone is confidence in themselves, to cheer them along and to inspire them.

How often do we see workplaces where employees don't want to be there, and they are miserable and the bosses complaining about not enough work being done? This is the greatest difference between a boss and a leader. Having those within your team working well together and enjoying showing up for what they do is important not just for a cohesive, productive team but for the overall wellbeing of those individuals and the organisation.

As leaders we will all face challenges, how we overcome them is what will set us aside. I never set out to be a leader and I never set out to be friends with my team and I always had boundaries, however I found my teams always respected that and me as their role model to look up to. We must always remember that how we deal with any challenges and obstacles as a leader that we are always being watched, and through this my leadership style has been to inspire others by staying fully engaged with communication as key throughout.

Effective communication should always be priority when leading a team, addressing challenges or issues immediately as they arise and providing clear direction and rationale throughout the process is important. Carefully considering the impact of your decisions, conveying and demonstrating the value in those decisions to your team is also as important so that they understand your reasoning for your decision. By doing this you are also helping them grow to be leaders as you're providing them with an insight into the holistic approach a leader needs to engage.

A collaborative approach within a team will always make a team stronger and enable them to often make smaller decisions or assist them in communicating a different approach to the task that they are working on. I recall once seeing the opportunity of connecting two very different areas to work towards solving a problem, and with a collaborative approach not only were the teams able to solve the problem, but it actually made them reassess all their systems to make them more streamlined and future proofed. This would not have happened without a collaborative approach and with encouragement from me as a leader to effectively communicate the need for both areas to discuss and evaluate their individual situations and what their visions were for the future of such projects. This has changed the way in which a process was carried out for decades to make it more functional, cost-effective and streamlined and inevitably has future proofed it for some time. As a leader I was privileged to see the joint problems from both areas and engage both to effectively work together towards a joint solution which neither would have known about or even thought about.

Inspiring your team to think outside the box is one of the most rewarding experiences we can have as leaders. To allow them to work out innovative solutions for common problems can often be life-changing – not just for them but for the organisation. As leaders we sometimes will lose the ability to see innovation in day-to-day processes. I've always enjoyed working with younger teams as their ideas, especially around digital solutions, can be innovative and increase productivity exponentially. Having clear communication lines allows your team to openly be able to offer their ideas and solutions which can be adapted or not. Feedback with your team is always important around any suggestions and decisions to allow them to continue feeling valued as a team member.

Being an effective leader is something that needs to be taken seriously, as a leader is not just a role model, but they are a mentor and someone who, if effective, is held in the highest regard. With this comes a level of influence that you can have on your team members. Guiding and mentoring your team to help them discover their potential as well as improving their performance whilst developing their skills and achieving their goals is important as a mentor to them. Showing them how a sympathetic leader can also be a strong supportive mentor and guide is more important that telling them how to do it.

Many of my team members who have considered me as their mentor and role model have gone on to have successful careers in their chosen fields and become leaders that I am proud of. As a leader this is my measure of success that I have allowed them to grow and be sympathetic but strong, engaged and encouraging. Where they have skills that they can identify behaviours that need to either be encouraged or discouraged and how to address this dependant on the issue through skills they have learnt, and I have modelled for them which can't be learnt but needs to be seen in action. Where they have a growth mindset for their team and that they have a leadership approach to encourage this. Where they have the knowledge that they are in turn impacting on their teams with everything they do and say. Where they can recognise and encourage those who have skills which need exploring further to follow them and guide them through. Where they recognise that team members all have different needs and wants and not all will want to achieve advancement and how to make the most of this within the team. Where they encourage open communication in safe and comfortable environments where their teams will effectively seek solutions, ask questions, request clarification and share their thoughts and needs.

For anyone aspiring to being a visionary leader or mentor I would say find those you admire, look at the qualities that you most admire in them, either ask them to be your mentor or work out how you can gain these qualities.

Visionary leaders are not scared to be challenged – one of my favourite sayings is 'challenge accepted', and I believe this attitude has seen me through, it has given me an approach to any problem as having a solution that just needs to be found. Qualities I'm sure they'll all have in common that they will be strong but approachable, have a highly communicative approach and consider all information that is put before them so that they are making a well-researched decision, they will be innovative and not afraid of embracing new innovative solutions, they will be encouraging and held in high regard by the teams they lead, they will be the glue that holds a team together and they will be the first person you want to share your ideas with.

I believe that anyone can learn to be a manager but to be a leader you need to be guided and follow in the footsteps of your mentors and other leaders that you admire – think what is it you value in high regard about them, what stands out about them that you would want to be a leader like them?

I believe that our impact is our legacy and the only real footprint we leave behind in this world. What others think of us is more important than what we think of ourselves so just imagine that those in your teams think of you highly and often speak highly of you long after you've left the organisation – what better can we leave behind through our leadership journey? As a leader I am always looking at challenging what we know and how can we make it better, I am not shy to adopt any new technology or embrace change, and I am driven to making the world a better place – even if that means one team at a time. Making others' lives better is the most rewarding thing we can do as a mentor or a leader.

# ABOUT ROBYN

ROBYN IS THE FOUNDER of Busy Connecting which specialises in business growth and development strategies.

Robyn's background is in multi-disciplinary marketing and communication specialising in key stakeholder and community engagement, with over forty years' experience in governance and compliance working on large strategic communication projects in both the corporate sector, government, and community in Australia and internationally. Her skills include writing legislative and government documentation, tenders, grants, government and corporate submissions, and strategic communication documentation. She now delivers these services to much smaller organisations, assisting businesses to grow and reach their full potential.

Driven to continue her personal mission advocating for women to raise their voices to reach full gender equality, Robyn is well known as being an advocate for funding for women.

Robyn has served on many committees and boards and is a passionate volunteer supporting domestic violence victims, homelessness and the environment. Robyn is a proud Gold Award Winner for Outstanding Community Support, AusMumpreneur Awards.

Robyn is a mentor for the Australian Women's Business School and International Day of the Girl Child. She has been a civic leader and is an advisor at the University of Sunshine Coast's Business Panel and a judge for many international awards.

# DR HASSAN YOUNES
# MY PASSION-DRIVEN LEADERSHIP
## NAVIGATING THE SPECTRUM OF EXCELLENCE

*If you stop improving when your competition doesn't, you will get left behind. So do you want to remain complacent or WIN?*

MY JOURNEY HAS BEEN nothing short of a thrilling adventure, one that has taken me through the dynamic realms of aerospace engineering, organisational change and business management. From my humble beginnings in the aerospace industry and the winding path I've travelled has brought me to where I stand today as a keynote speaker, number-one bestselling author and successful serial entrepreneur.

It all began with the kind of passion that stirs in the heart of a young, eager teenager – the skies and airplanes held a magnetic fascination for me. From the very moment I gazed upon the sleek, soaring machines that traversed the boundless blue, I knew that my destiny was intertwined with the world of aerospace. The yearning in my heart for the skies ignited a relentless ambition that would propel me on a journey like no other.

With an unwavering vision and mission firmly set, I embarked on a quest to cultivate a career within the aerospace industry. It was a path marked by challenges, a journey where dedication would be tested time and again. Pursuing a degree in aerospace engineering was no easy feat, but my determination knew no bounds; it was clear that this was the only path meant for me.

The halls of academia became my sanctuary as I delved into the complexities of aerospace engineering. Hours of study and dedication paved the way for my journey to the stars. Armed with knowledge and a degree in aerospace engineering, I took my first steps into the professional realm, ready to contribute my skills and passion to the industry.

My journey led me to the Australian Department of Defence, where I was entrusted with responsibilities that were both challenging and rewarding. This was where I honed my skills, further fuelling my passion for aviation and innovation. However, my pursuit of excellence did not stop there.

The next chapter of my career unfolded as I embarked on an incredible opportunity: joining the esteemed ranks of Boeing Commercial Airplanes in Melbourne, Australia. Here, I was part of a team dedicated to crafting the future of aviation, contributing my expertise to the intricate world of aircraft design and development.

In retrospect, it's clear that my journey was a testament to the power of unwavering passion, resilience in the face of adversity and the indomitable spirit of ambition. From the moment my fascination with airplanes took root in my teenage heart to my professional involvement with industry giants, it has been a journey marked by the pursuit of dreams among the clouds and the unwavering commitment to a career that truly soars.

As I traversed the early stages of my career in the aerospace industry, my journey took an unexpected turn, driven by my curiosity, adaptability and a passion for innovation. While my heart remained firmly in the aerospace realm, I found myself drawn towards uncharted territories, captivated by the idea of exploring diverse industries beyond my aerospace career.

Amidst the hum of jet engines and the world of aerospace engineering, a new passion was silently incubating within me – the passion to lead, to steer the course of an organisation and to chart the path for a thriving business. It was a yearning that went beyond my professional pursuits; it was a vision of creating a flexible lifestyle for my young family, one that offered comfort and financial security.

Balancing my full-time role in the aerospace industry with this new-found ambition was no small feat. However, fuelled by an unyielding desire to provide my family with a life unburdened by financial constraints, I embarked on a parallel journey. This venture was more than just a business operation; it was a manifestation of my passion, a quest for financial flexibility and the pursuit of a life without bounds or restrictions.

The road was far from easy; it demanded sacrifices, sleepless nights and relentless determination. Yet, it was the fire of ambition, the thrill of innovation and the unwavering support of my family that sustained me. With each step forward, my vision of a lifestyle marked by comfort and financial freedom became increasingly tangible.

As I balanced my responsibilities in the aerospace industry with my entrepreneurial pursuits, I realised that this journey was not just about financial gain. It was a testament to the power of passion and the resilience of the human spirit. It was a journey that taught me that with dedication and a clear vision, one could indeed bridge the gap between aspiration and reality.

As the chapters of my professional journey unfolded, each new business venture we established marked a profound learning experience in the realm of entrepreneurship. These ventures ranged from vocational training organisations, where we aimed to empower individuals with essential skills, to the exhilarating world of travel agencies, where we helped people explore the globe. Each venture was a unique voyage of discovery, presenting invaluable lessons in the art of entrepreneurship.

With every endeavour, my passion for entrepreneurship burgeoned, becoming an unwavering flame that flickered beyond any reasonable doubt. It was a passion so intense that it became abundantly clear: the time had come to take a life-altering decision. I chose to officially retire from my aerospace career, a move that would transform me into a full-time serial entrepreneur.

This transition was not merely a shift in career path; it was a leap into the unknown, fuelled by the boundless fervour to explore uncharted territories. With the aerospace industry as my foundation, I embarked on a journey to fully embrace my role as an entrepreneur, an endeavour that was as thrilling as it was challenging.

My passion for entrepreneurship led me to venture even further, transcending geographical boundaries and cultural landscapes. I set my sights on establishing an international education facility in the Philippines, driven by the belief that education knows no borders. It was an ambitious endeavour, one that demanded not only dedication but also a strong commitment to fostering global learning opportunities for disadvantaged families and their children.

Moreover, the entrepreneurial spirit within led me to navigate the intricate world of investment and property development projects right here in Australia. These ventures introduced me to the exhilarating power of calculated risk-taking, where every decision had the potential to shape the trajectory of my businesses. Operating multiple successful businesses simultaneously became a testament to the capacity of passion and dedication to transcend limitations.

In the tapestry of my career, these endeavours represent not just financial pursuits but a manifestation of my commitment to my entrepreneurial dreams. They were a testament to the power of calculated risk-taking, strategic planning and relentless dedication to managing diverse businesses effectively.

The quest for education and knowledge was a flame that burned ever brighter, especially when it came to the dynamics of business and leadership. It was a passion that knew no bounds, an unquenchable thirst for understanding the intricacies of these domains. With each new educational pursuit, I delved deeper into the world of business and leadership, driven by an unyielding desire to expand my horizons.

My educational journey was marked by relentless dedication and a commitment to excellence. I pursued and achieved multiple tertiary qualifications, creating a solid foundation upon which I would build my expertise. These qualifications spanned business, business administration and leadership and management, representing a multifaceted approach to understanding the complexities of the business world.

The culmination of my educational journey was the attainment of a doctorate in business administration, a pinnacle achievement that solidified my expertise in the field. Armed with this prestigious qualification and a trove of complementary diploma certifications in business management, accounting and education, I was more than prepared to navigate the ever-evolving challenges of leadership in the business sector.

My passion for education had transformed me into a credible expert and thought leader in the business sector. I was no longer a passive learner; I had become a dynamic contributor to the discourse surrounding business strategies, leadership principles and the nuances of effective management.

Today, I stand as a professional speaker, poised to share the wealth of knowledge and expertise I've accumulated over the years with a global audience. My mission is clear: to deliver powerful, knowledgeable strategies, expert advice and impactful keynotes that resonate with individuals and organisations worldwide. It is a role that allows me to inspire, motivate and empower others to embrace the transformative power of education and leadership in the pursuit of excellence.

As I step onto the stage as a professional speaker, I carry with me the legacy of my passion for education and knowledge. It is a legacy that continues to evolve, a testament to the enduring belief that education is the cornerstone of progress and that sharing knowledge is a noble endeavour. In this role, I find fulfilment in not only expanding my own horizons but also in guiding others on their journeys toward success and enlightenment in the ever-evolving landscape of business and leadership.

My journey as a passionate leader is an ongoing odyssey, a relentless pursuit of growth, impact and boundless aspiration. Today, I don multiple hats, each emblematic of my commitment to leadership and my insatiable desire to shape a brighter future. These roles extend across multiple business organisations, both in Australia and abroad, a testament to the depth of my dedication and the breadth of my ambitions.

As the CEO, managing director and chairman of these diverse entities, I find myself at the helm of an intricate web of responsibilities. Each role carries with it a unique set of challenges and opportunities, demanding a profound understanding of leadership dynamics and an unwavering commitment to the causes I champion.

These multifaceted roles are more than just titles; they represent a profound commitment to making a positive impact on the world. With each hat I wear, I am entrusted with the responsibility to steer organisations toward success and prosperity, all while remaining true to my core values of integrity, innovation and unwavering dedication to a global community.

My passion knows no boundaries, no reasonable limits. It is an unquenchable fire that propels me to bridge the ever-widening gap between the needs, wants and educational desires of consumers worldwide. It is my belief that passionate leadership has the power to deliver what no other organisation or leader can – the ability to uplift and empower our global community in ways that transcend mere business.

To me, passionate leadership is not just a role, it's a calling – a calling to redefine the way organisations interact with their communities, to foster deeper connections and to drive positive change on a global scale. It is a commitment to go beyond the expected, to push boundaries and to pave the way for a future where the unattainable becomes achievable.

There are three pieces of advice that I would give to any business leader or emerging business leader:

**Embrace multifaceted leadership:** This involves a leader to willingly take on diverse roles and responsibilities within and beyond their core expertise. The benefits are that it broadens perspective, fosters adaptability and enhances decision-making.

**Pursue passion with purpose:** As a business leader, align your deepest passions with a clear, meaningful goal. This clarity fuels resilience, amplifies impact and fosters fulfilment. It transforms abstract dreams into achievable, purpose-driven actions, enabling you to make a lasting difference in your life and the lives of others.

**Lead beyond boundaries:** Every leader must lead beyond reasonable boundaries. Your commitment to bridging the gap between needs, wants and educational desires for consumers globally showcases the transformative power of visionary leadership.

In conclusion, my journey as a passionate leader continues to unfold, guided by an unquenchable desire to create a world where leadership is synonymous with empowerment, innovation and boundless potential. With each role I undertake, I am propelled by the belief that, as a passionate leader, I can contribute to shaping a world where the aspirations of individuals and communities are not just met but exceeded. It is a journey defined by ambition, dedication and an unyielding commitment to making a positive impact on the global stage.

As I reflect on this transformative phase of my life, I am reminded that passion, coupled with the courage to embrace change, can unlock a world of opportunities. My professional journey is a testament to the extraordinary potential that lies within each of us to pursue our passions and embark on ventures that push the boundaries of what we can achieve. It is a reminder that with each step we take into the unknown, we have the chance to discover new horizons and redefine the limits of our potential.

# ABOUT DR HASSAN

Dr Hassan Younes is an international keynote speaker, author and a serial entrepreneur.

He has a background in aerospace engineering, organisational change and business management across multiple diverse industries, and over two decades in the education and training sector.

Dr Hassan Younes holds a doctorate in business administration (leadership and management), an honours degree in aerospace and other qualifications in business administration, business management, accounting and education.

Throughout his professional career, Dr Hassan Younes has utilised his skills and experience in business management to build a successful vocational training organisation, multiple travel agencies, build an international education facility in the Philippines and managed investment and property development projects.

Dr Hassan Younes is also the founder and chair of the International Academy of Marawi, managing director at Caradon Investments, founder and senior business coach for Lanao Business Services and is the managing director at Arndell Park Early Childhood Learning Centre.

# DR SARIFA ALONTO-YOUNES
# ORPHANHOOD TO PASSIONATE VISIONARY LEADING
## THE TRANSFORMATIVE POWER OF EDUCATION

*Change your perspective and find the freedom to succeed.*

IN THE SPHERE OF leadership, there exists a rare breed of individuals who transcend the ordinary – a breed driven by an insatiable passion to envision and create a better world. They are the torchbearers of change, the architects of the future and the embodiments of what we call 'passionate visionary leadership'.

Within the vast landscape of leadership, there is a unique and transformative dimension that I've had the privilege to both witness and embody throughout my journey – a dimension I'm eager to share with you in this chapter.

My life's narrative has been interwoven with threads of fearless dreams and an unwavering belief in the extraordinary potential of passionate visionary leadership. It's a belief that stems from my own experiences, from humble beginnings to the milestones and challenges that have shaped me into the leader I am today.

In these pages, I will embark on a deeply personal exploration, sharing the lessons learned, the triumphs celebrated and the countless obstacles faced along the way. It's a journey that has taught me that leadership is not merely a role but a state of being – a commitment to a vision that burns with an unquenchable fire.

My aspiration is that, as we navigate this chapter together, you will discover insights and inspiration that resonate with your own leadership aspirations. I firmly believe that every individual has the potential to become a passionate visionary leader, capable of catalysing positive change in their lives, their organisations and the world.

## EARLY LIFE: A TALE OF RESILIENCE

My path to visionary leadership was paved with obstacles, which others may label as insurmountable adversity, from the very beginning. The loss of my father when I was a tender three-year-old, followed by the heartbreaking departure of my mother at the age of ten, were undoubtedly the most devastating experiences I had ever endured (I shared in detail in my first book, *Love Your Obstacles)*. Yet, they became the crucible that shaped my life, transforming those hardships into stepping stones toward a brighter future.

Imagine being a child, thrust into an ocean of uncertainty where swimming was a foreign language and survival felt like a distant dream. There were no instructors, no life jackets, no prior lessons on how to navigate those tumultuous waters. At first, I flailed and struggled desperately just to stay afloat, to survive. But gradually, through sheer determination, an unwavering spirit and insatiable thirst for learning, I not only learned to swim but emerged from those turbulent waters stronger, with resilience, confidence and courage I never thought possible. Being orphaned became my unchosen training ground, equipping me with the tools I needed to confront the reality that lay ahead.

Those heartbreaking losses could have cast me into a never-ending despair, but I made a conscious decision to forge a different path. Even in my darkest moments, when all I had to hold onto were my prayers, hope and dreams, the enduring wisdom of my mother echoed in my heart: *Education will drag you out of misery.* Those words became my unwavering creed, I clung to the belief that knowledge held the key to my future. My mother's wisdom resonated deeply within me, sparking a relentless pursuit of education.

For those who read my story, I want you to know this: Life's most trying moments, its harshest trials, can become the catalysts for profound transformation. Even when hope seems distant and the journey ahead appears treacherous, remember that deep within you resides an untapped reservoir of strength and determination. In the face of obstacles, embrace your inner courage and let it guide you towards the visionary leader you were born to become.

Yes, your journey may be fraught with obstacles, but it is through these very trials that your character is refined and your potential unlocked. Hold steadfast to your unshakable faith in yourself, your unwavering resilience and your unshakeable belief in the transformative power of education. As you tread your path, understand that every obstacle, every setback, is an opportunity in disguise – a chance to rise above and become the inspiring leader you were destined to be. Learn to embrace your obstacles, for they are the raw materials from which you will craft your own unique and inspiring destiny.

## THE TRANSFORMATIVE POWER OF EDUCATION

It was through the ardent belief in the transformative power of education that I found my way forward. It was a belief that surged within me like a relentless tempest, a belief that would not only shape the trajectory of my life but ignite the spirits of countless others I encountered on my journey.

The first few years after I lost my father was like being cast adrift in a turbulent sea, yearning for the shores of knowledge. I just couldn't wait to go to school seeing my mother struggling to make ends meet. Where she would say, her voice like an anthem of hope, 'If I had a formal education, it would be easier to acquire a decent job that can raise a family comfortably and with dignity.' Hearing my mother repetitively emphasising the power of education. These words, spoken in the quiet moments of our lives, became etched into my very soul, instilling a love for education that burned brighter with each passing day. Education became my refuge, solace and beacon of hope accompanied by my prayers.

In the words of Nelson Mandela, 'Education is the most powerful weapon which you can use to change the world.' It was through this profound realisation that I embarked on a journey, determined to seize the weapon of knowledge and wield it not only for personal transformation but for the betterment of my community and beyond.

I can still feel the weight of grief on the day I lost my mother. It was during our examination week, a time when the world seemed to crumble around me. Compassionate teachers extended their hands, offering separate examinations to take place couple of weeks after our scheduled examination period as a special consideration so I get a chance to prepare, understanding the turmoil within my heart and what I was going through. But I refused their offer, for I was determined not to be marked by my grief and toil under the weight of special treatment. I didn't want to be treated special because of the death of my mother. Also, I didn't want to give my teachers extra work and burden to formulate new questions that could be harder than what they had designed for everyone else in the class. So, with tears almost immersing and staining my textbooks and notebooks, I ended up preparing for the exams, studying harder than anyone else in my class in the midst of my mourning during the wake of my mother. I didn't even have that moment to grieve as I immersed myself in my studies.

In the words of Albert Einstein, 'Imagination is more important than knowledge. For knowledge is limited, whereas imagination embraces the entire world.' My imagination soared, fuelled by the power of education, and I realised that it held the key not only to my personal dreams but to the dreams of countless others who were facing adversity.

Pages of my textbooks and notebooks, soaked in both sorrow and determination, clung together as though bearing witness to my relentless commitment. There were times I would have difficulty separating and flipping pages. Day and night, I immersed myself in my studies, my mother's wisdom echoing in every word I read. With dedication, commitment and prayers I not only passed those exams but soared to the pinnacle, securing the coveted position of TOP 1 in our grade level and ultimately graduated as the valedictorian of grade six.

With hard work I learned how to study harder and obtained scholarship throughout my studies. In those moments, I discovered the undeniable truth in my mother's words – education had the remarkable ability to breathe life into my dreams. It's a realisation that education was not merely a tool for self-advancement but a profound means to uplift those who are often left in the shadows and be a catalyst for change, a force capable of transforming the lives of countless others.

## A DREAM TO INSPIRE

Rising from the shadows of adversity, I nurtured dreams that transcended the boundaries of my own life. These dreams were not mere aspirations for personal achievement but a fervent desire to extend a hand to those who had been marginalised by fate – disadvantaged children, orphans and women facing insurmountable odds. I envisioned a world where education could be the bridge out of despair and into a life of sustainability and contribution. My lived experiences and own journey fuelled my passion to ensure that others could escape the cycle of adversity, just as I had.

In the words of the ever-inspiring Angela F Williams, the president and chief executive of United Way Worldwide, when asked by Forbes what advice she could offer to women aspiring to take on leadership roles, she replied with profound wisdom: 'Don't be afraid of failure.' She encouraged women not to allow obstacles to deter them, but rather, to remain observant, resilient and resourceful in finding alternative paths to overcome challenges. Angela underscores that hearing 'no' should not be a deterrent but rather an invitation to persist and thrive.

As I embark on my journey toward my dreams, I carry Angela's words with me as a beacon of guidance. They are a testament to the unwavering spirit of individuals who dare to dream and aspire to inspire. Much like her, I refuse to let fear hold me back, and I vow to never be complacent in the face of adversity. Instead, I will seek new avenues, tirelessly and relentlessly, until my dreams of uplifting the marginalised and providing a beacon of hope to those in need become a glorious reality.

The path ahead may be challenging, but it is in these very challenges that the fire of inspiration burns brighter. For it is not enough to dream; we must also have the courage to act. Let these words be a testament to the power of resilience and the unwavering commitment to making a difference, one dream at a time.

Allow me to share a story when I was about to venture into the world of entrepreneurship armed with nothing but a vision, a young toddler named Adam to care for and sheer determination. When my husband, Hassan, and I made the audacious decision to embark on this entrepreneurial journey, we did so with hearts full of courage and pockets devoid of financial capital.

It was a very courageous move to venture a medium-size business without any financial capacity to start with. Imagine the circumstances: My husband, was tirelessly dedicated to his full-time job at Boeing Australia, while I found myself in the unfamiliar terrain of Australia, armed with nothing more than my education and the burning desire to create something meaningful.

Hassan, recognising the need to balance our responsibilities, made me aware that I had to manage the day-to-day operation of the business as he was working full-time and could not be with me. He posed a question that would become a defining moment in our journey: 'CAN YOU DO IT?' Without a moment of hesitation, I replied with a resounding 'YES!' He then added, 'ARE YOU SURE?' I then replied that, 'Being an orphan was the scariest journey I had. With you by my side I'm not scared of failure as I have a shoulder to lean on if worse comes to worst.'

My past, marked by the loss of my parents, had already instilled in me a tenacious spirit. But it was having Hassan as my anchor, my unwavering support, that emboldened me to face the unknown, unafraid of the possibility of failure.

To start with my entrepreneurship journey, we approached every bank in Melbourne to support us with our business venture and each of them turned as away with a resounding 'NO' straight to our faces. They dismissed our dreams without even glancing at our meticulously crafted business plan. The word 'NO' echoed in our ears, a deafening rejection that would have deterred many. I was convinced that alternative paths existed, waiting to be discovered.

In the face of adversity, I refused to give up to the weight of rejection. Turning to Hassan, I told him that 'there must be other ways out there'.

Our journey was far from over. Each 'NO' we encountered served as a fuel for our determination. It reaffirmed our belief that with unwavering commitment, boundless resilience and an unshakeable faith in our dreams, we could surmount any obstacle. This chapter of our lives stands as a testament to the remarkable capacity of the human spirit to transcend adversity, to find a way even when all doors seem closed.

Our story serves as a reminder that sometimes the greatest challenges lead to the most extraordinary victories. With courage, unwavering support and an unshakable belief in oneself, we can turn every 'NO' into a stepping stone on the path to our dreams.

After two days of enduring those rejections, I couldn't help but wonder if my headscarf, a symbol of my identity, was inadvertently becoming a stumbling block. Frustration and desperation gripped our spirits, prompting me to suggest to my husband that he meet with an area manager from Commonwealth Bank (CBA) alone, without my presence. It was a difficult decision, but I couldn't shake the feeling that perhaps my appearance was affecting our chances.

Fast-forward to a moment of ingenious thinking. We devised a plan to contact CBA and request a meeting with one of their area managers to take place at our home after 6pm. The idea was to create a more relaxed, personal atmosphere where we could present our case in a less formal setting.

Our persistence bore fruit, and on a fateful evening, Nick, like a beacon of hope, arrived on our doorstep at 7pm. What transpired in the following thirty minutes was nothing short of magical. We poured our hearts into our words, sharing our dreams and ambitions, and weaving a vivid tapestry of the child care and kindergarten facilities we envisioned. Nick listened intently, not just to our words, but to the passion and unwavering commitment that infused every syllable. Our vision was not just a business plan; it was a dream rooted in the belief in the transformative power of education, particularly in early childhood development.

Armed with little more than AUD$3,745 in our bank account, a sum that serendipitously coincided with a payday from my husband's work at Boeing, we laid bare our dreams. It was a moment that teetered on the edge of uncertainty. But Nick saw something in us, something beyond the numbers on a balance sheet. He recognised our determination, our belief and our potential to make a lasting impact on the community. He understood that sometimes, dreams require more than financial backing; they require champions who believe in them wholeheartedly.

In a remarkable turn of events, Nick approved the amount of money we needed to realise our dream of constructing and establishing the child care and kindergarten facilities. It was not just a financial grant; it was a validation of our determination, a testament to the strength of our vision and an affirmation of the boundless potential of education.

This chapter in our journey reminds us of the words of Winston Churchill: 'Success is not final; failure is not fatal: It is the courage to continue that counts.' In the face of rejection, we found the courage to persist, to think unconventionally and to believe in the transformative power of our dreams. It reaffirms the notion that, with passion and perseverance, even the most audacious dreams can find their way to reality.

Angela's words resonate like a powerful symphony, reminding us that the word 'NO' need not be a barrier but rather a stepping stone on our journey to success. Her wisdom strikes at the heart of a truth we often forget: obstacles, no matter how imposing they may seem, are never insurmountable. Instead, they are invitations to explore alternative paths, to seek out creative solutions and to rise above adversity with unwavering determination.

Angela's assertion that 'NO' is merely a word struck a chord deep within me. It's a truth that every woman, every dreamer, should etch into their very souls. Too often, we allow 'NO' to be accompanied by a heavy emotional burden, one that threatens to crush our spirit and dampen our dreams. But, in reality, 'NO' is just a word, devoid of power unless we choose to imbue it with meaning.

When I ventured into the world of entrepreneurship, my heart was drawn to the field of education. The dream of establishing a child care centre and kindergarten facilities, where not only my own children but also the offspring of hardworking parents could receive high-quality care and education, had been a passion that ignited my soul. It was a dream rooted in a desire to serve, to provide job opportunities for the community and to create a space where children could flourish.

My passion for education soared to new heights with the arrival of my fourth child, Dania, who, at the tender age of eleven, became a published author. Her journey became a source of inspiration, driving me to expand my educational endeavours beyond borders, establishing educational institutions in both Australia and the Philippines. This expansion allowed me to touch the lives of numerous children and students, granting them access to quality education that empowers, nurtures and helps them find their rightful place in the world.

With each passing day, my commitment to education grows stronger. It's a testament to the profound impact education can have on individuals and communities alike. It's a reminder that our dreams, when fuelled by unwavering passion and the belief in the transformative power of education, have the capacity to not only thrive but to empower others to thrive alongside us.

The establishment of several educational institutions has not only fulfilled our dreams but has also enabled my family and me to extend a helping hand to marginalised women, disadvantaged children and orphans, addressing not only their educational needs but also their basic necessities. Today, as we embark on a journey of expansion, our commitment to aiding underprivileged individuals, both locally and globally, knows no bounds. With the formal registration of our foundation, the ALONTO-YOUNES FOUNDATION, INC, we are poised to effect transformative change in the lives of countless individuals, empowering them to reach their full potential.

## AN INSPIRATIONAL JOURNEY UNFOLDS

In the tapestry of my life, woven with threads of unwavering determination and an unyielding belief in the transformative power of education, I forged a path that defied the odds. From the tender roots of orphanhood, I grew into a resilient individual who, against all odds, blossomed into a visionary and award-winning author, entrepreneur, author, international speaker, TEDx speaker and a compassionate philanthropist.

My journey is not just a story; it's a testament to the incredible capacity of the human spirit. It's a story of how hard work, relentless dedication and an unwavering commitment to my dreams allowed me to rise above the challenges life placed in my path. I am living proof that adversity can be transformed into opportunity and that our past need not define our future.

I firmly believe that the foundation of my entrepreneurial endeavours, my inspiring speaking engagements, my far-reaching philanthropic programs and my enduring literary legacy lies in the education I received. Education wasn't just a privilege; it was the cornerstone of my transformation. It equipped me with the knowledge, the resilience and the courage to turn my dreams into reality.

I am not merely a beneficiary of the power of education; I am its fervent advocate. I have witnessed firsthand how education has the unparalleled potential to illuminate the darkest corners of despair, to empower the most vulnerable among us and to pave the way for a brighter, more hopeful future. My journey is a living testament to the boundless possibilities that education offers to those who dare to dream and believe in their dreams.

As I continue to walk this inspiring path, I carry with me the unwavering belief that no dream is too audacious, no challenge too daunting and no obstacle too insurmountable. My story is a reminder to all that with passion, perseverance and an unwavering commitment to the power of education, we can not only transform our own lives but also inspire others to reach for the stars and realise their true potential.

I don't share this journey to boast, but to humbly illustrate the transformative power of determination and the profound impact of education. It's a reminder that no matter where one starts, it's the relentless pursuit of dreams and an unshakable belief in the promise of education that can lead us to remarkable heights. As I continue on this path, I strive to inspire others to dare to dream, to believe in themselves and to embrace the life-altering magic of education – force that can illuminate even the darkest of paths and empower individuals to not only transform their own lives but to uplift others along the way.

## CONCLUSION

As you close this chapter and carry these lessons forward, remember that each of us has the potential to become a passionate visionary leader, igniting positive change in our spheres of influence and beyond. The path may be challenging, but with the fire of passion, the strength of purpose and the obstacles to overcome, we can shape a brighter future for ourselves and for the world.

From my own experiences, we've learned that an obstacle is not a roadblock but a stepping stone, that 'NO' is just a word until we give it power and that education is the cornerstone of transformation.

And through the stories and wisdom shared, we've uncovered lessons that can guide us all on our own paths of passionate visionary leadership:

**Transform obstacle**: obstacle is not a barrier but a catalyst for growth. It has the potential to transform us into stronger, more resilient leaders. Embrace challenges as opportunities to learn and adapt.

**Reframe rejection**: The word 'NO' is not a dead-end but a detour. Use rejection as a chance to explore alternative routes, innovate and persist in the pursuit of your vision.

**Empower through education**: Education is not just a personal asset; it's a force for societal change. Invest in knowledge and advocate for education as a means to empower others and uplift entire communities.

**Fan the flames of passion**: Passion is the driving force behind visionary leadership. Let your passion fuel your dreams, infusing every action with purpose and determination.

**Nurture your vision**: A powerful vision has the potential to inspire and move mountains. Hold onto your dreams with unwavering belief, knowing that your determination will pave the way.

**Lead to inspire and serve**: True leadership is not about authority but about inspiring and serving others. Use your leadership as a force for positive change, uplifting those around you and making a lasting impact.

# ABOUT DR SARIFA

DR SARIFA ALONTO-YOUNES IS a serial entrepreneur, number-one best-selling author, an international speaker, a philanthropist and an international speaker.

She has been featured in various media outlets. Sarifa is also the author of the book *Love your Obstacles.*

A passionate advocate for women's empowerment and female entrepreneurship, Dr Sarifa speaks regularly at conferences around the world on these topics. She is also involved with various charities that focus on helping disadvantaged families, empowering women and orphan children in need.

Sarifa's mission is to help as many people as possible achieve their dreams and live their best lives. She is passionate about helping entrepreneurs start and grow their businesses, and believes that when women succeed, societies thrive.

An international speaker, Dr Sarifa Alonto-Younes travels the world sharing her insights on education, female entrepreneurship, leadership and women's empowerment. She is also passionate about giving back; she supports a number of charities that help children in need.

Be the captain of your life and direct your ship in the direction you desire, even in stormy weather.

## HER EDUCATION

Dr Sarifa Alonto-Younes holds a doctorate in education, a master's degree in industrial and organisational psychology, a master's degree in education and training and a bachelor's degree in psychology, which have made her a strong voice on international stages speaking on organisational change, social behaviours and personal empowerment.

## PROFESSIONAL CAREER

Sarifa Alonto Younes is a certified NLP practitioner and business consultants. She is the president and founder of the International Academy of Marawi (IAM), Philippines; director and co-founder of Training College of Australia; CEO and founder of Arndell Park Early Childhood Learning Centre, Australia. She is also the director of Lanao Business Services.

## ALEX SY
# UNLEASHING THE LEADER WITHIN
## MY JOURNEY OF EMPATHY AND INSPIRATION

*I measure my impact in the transformative lives of those I've touched,
the sustenance of growing businesses and the elevation of individuals to
their highest potential.*

ALLOW ME TO INVITE you into the intricate tapestry of my life, one woven with threads of leadership, resilience and unwavering commitment. I am Mr Alex Sy, and my story is a testament to the belief that leaders are not just made, they are born, with a spark waiting to be ignited.

### ORIGINS AND EARLY INSIGHTS
Born in the heart of Cebu City, Philippines, I embarked on a transformative journey when my family migrated to Australia during my formative years. Settling in Victoria, I found myself at University High School in Parkville. It was here that I first sensed the latent leadership qualities within me, a realisation that leadership wasn't something I acquired – it was part of who I am.

### LESSONS FROM THE PAST
As I navigated through life, my father emerged as my cornerstone of inspiration. His success as a revered businessman in the Philippines left an indelible mark on my psyche. Observing his leadership in organisations like Rotary, Lions Club and Chinese Business Associations instilled in me the significance of leading through service and dedication.

Beyond my father's influence, I sought inspiration from the stories of successful leaders who led by example. Their journeys, their achievements and the respect they commanded among peers, communities and families fuelled my aspirations.

## IGNITING PASSION THROUGH ACTION

My fervour for leadership blossomed during my Philippine childhood, where I excelled in dirt bike racing at a tender age of nine. A call from my local community and friends to lead, teach and champion them in races reinforced my innate capacity to guide.

Transitioning to Australia, (still in the Philippines) I embraced the Boy Scouts at ten yrs old and swiftly ascended from Squad Leader to Squadron Leader, tasked with leading five squads at a Boy Scout Jamboree. This juncture illuminated the profound influence of a leader, highlighting the willingness of others to follow when trust and respect are earned.

## DEFINING MOMENTS IN MELBOURNE

My high school years in Melbourne mirrored my innate leadership flair. Elected as a student representative to the School Council, I became the voice of my peers, advocating for their needs. My captaincy in basketball and volleyball, leadership in the school's debating team and triumphs in swimming competitions underscored my multifaceted leadership prowess.

My commitment to community service was unwavering. I played an integral role in establishing multicultural community groups, emceed diverse events and even served on the Bendigo Community Bank Board. Guiding Mentored Filipino international students, acting as a multicultural ambassador and assuming the presidency of non-profit organisations showcased my dedication to making a meaningful impact to the community

At a mere twenty years old, I was bestowed the responsibility of a

Neighborhood Watch Area Coordinator, reinforcing my commitment to community safety, and my commitment as a community leader.

## SURMOUNTING OBSTACLES AND EMBRACING EMPATHY

My Asian ethnicity presented formidable challenges, provoking apprehension about how my directions leadership styles would be perceived. Yet, I confronted these biases apprehensions head-on by embracing a consultative and empathetic approach. This hallmark style became my compass for effective leadership – leading by example and fostering an environment of empathy.

I transitioned seamlessly from tasks as varied as cleaning, driving and clerical duties, channelling this ability to pivot into a trait of profound listening. My blend of skills, experience and hands-on management shaped a team that respected me for my leadership, transcending outward appearances.

My pride in my Asian heritage and accomplishments as a respected leader empowered me to transcend adversity through life skills, experiences and a willingness to listen.

## GUIDING PRINCIPLES AND ETHICAL LEADERSHIP

My leadership style is a symphony of empathy and lead by example. My guiding principles are elegantly simple: Respect is a two-way street, earned rather than bestowed. My journey led me to become a respected leader within the communities that I served in my Filipino community in Victoria, fuelled by the art of listening, rewarding hard work, rational decision-making, perseverance and gratitude for inspiration derived from my father and successful figures.

## FORGING COLLABORATION THROUGH CONSULTATION

My leadership essence is rooted in a consultative approach, valuing diverse perspectives and soliciting opinions, culminating in a shared journey toward outcomes and objectives. Yet, when necessity dictates, I stand assertive, making decisions that steer the ship.

A remarkable instance was my appointment as the inaugural general manager for a food distribution company. Amid a sea of applicants, I stood as the lone Asian. The company faced fiscal turbulence, plummeting sales and dire cash flow. Amidst these challenges, I orchestrated a BBQ luncheon, transparently detailing our situation and the road to recovery. A culture of cross-departmental collaboration birthed solutions, propelling the company toward profitability.

## INNOVATION AMIDST ADVERSITY

The year 2020 brought unprecedented challenges with the COVID-19 pandemic, reshaping my vision. My aspiration to excel in a senior corporate role shifted. Adapting to the evolving landscape, I established my own business offering consulting and mentoring services. This venture harnessed the transformative power of collaboration and innovation, steering businesses toward growth amid adversity.

## DRAWING WISDOM FROM MENTORS AND INSPIRATION

Beyond my personal experiences, I found profound inspiration in the narratives of great leaders – learning from their journeys, their triumphs and their struggles. My father's work ethic remains an enduring influence, shaping my perspective on myself and others.

An accidental encounter with an elderly businessman during a rainy night unfolded as destiny's design. His mentorship wove into my narrative, guiding me in life, business, community and people. Our bond, spanning over two decades, epitomised the transformative power of mentorship.

Guiding the next generation, I mentored a budding chef and restaurateur, nurturing his leadership identity. His evolution into an empathetic, decisive and empowering visionary leader ignited my excitement for his journey.

## CREATING A LEGACY OF EMPOWERMENT

My legacy finds its essence in tangible results – goal achievements and strategic progress. It resonates in my standing as a respected community member, business leader and mentor. I measure my impact in the transformative lives of those I've touched, the sustenance of growing businesses and the elevation of individuals to their highest potential.

## A GLIMPSE INTO THE FUTURE

To aspiring visionary leaders, my advice is distilled in a symphony of virtues: empathy, active listening, humble example-setting, effective communication, positive outlook, mutual respect, unwavering integrity, clear decisiveness, collaborative spirit and goal-oriented focus.

These principles paved the path of my journey, resonating in the heart of my leadership philosophy.

## GRATITUDE AND HUMILITY

I stand humbled by the gifts bestowed upon me – the ability to lead, inspire and adapt. These skills, forged through life's highs and lows, were nurtured by observing diverse leadership styles. My commitment to empathy and collaboration is unwavering. My passion is rooted in empowering individuals to rise to greatness.

Reflecting on my journey since childhood, the flame of leadership was always ablaze within me, yet I chose to remain grounded. As I embark on a new role as president of a non-profit organisation, advocating against loneliness and social isolation, I affirm that leadership is a birthright – an innate quality that transcends outward circumstances.

Leadership isn't merely about issuing directives – it's about illuminating the path and demonstrating how.

# ABOUT ALEX

ALEX SY IS THE managing director of Atlas Business Consulting & Mentoring Services which is based in Melbourne, Victoria, Australia. He has had over thirty-five years of hands-on experience in senior management and is a board adviser in small and medium-sized businesses.

He named his company, Atlas Business Consulting & Mentoring, after his family's business in Cebu, which is Cebu Atlas Hardware. He did this to honour his father's legacy.

His passion and what fulfils him is to share his knowledge for the main aim of improving a business or a person. He also owned small businesses in the past and truly understands the challenges and journey small business owners go through.

He has leveraged his broad range of experience across several industries as well as cross-departmental functions. He shares his knowledge and experience with clients from his active roles on several boards in not-for-profit organisations, business councils, SMEs, as well as community and multicultural organisations.

Alex has developed great connections with people based on mutual respect, trust and values. He is an effective facilitator and mediator and has people management skills.

Alex focuses on key outcomes for his clients in the areas of improving business performance, managing growth and change, business sustainability, leadership and new business startups. Whilst he focuses on his client's business growth, Alex also focuses on the people within to ensure there's team culture, spirit, motivation and a positive mindset.

Alex is passionate about helping businesses grow and remain sustainable. His mantra is: Always think and stay positive, and empower people to become effective leaders.

# JASON CORDI
# DIVERSE COMMUNITY LEADERSHIP

*Put yourself out there and try different things. It is a risk worth taking if you want to become a leader in your field.*

BEING OF SERVICE TO the community has been the source of immense joy and happiness in life for me. And it is through supporting the community that has embraced me during my upbringing that led to the discovery of my passion and eventual journey to become a visionary leader.

In September 2019, I began the honourable role of editor-in-chief of Australia's Filipino newspaper, *The Philippine Times*. *The Philippine Times* was founded in 1990 and is the only Filipino newspaper in Victoria and also Australia's longest-serving Filipino publication.

At the time, I was working full-time as a career librarian, a role which I've enjoyed since completing my Bachelor of Business (Information and Knowledge Management) in 2012. Today, I continue to give myself fully to both roles, and it's in my role as editor-in-chief where I've been recognised as an advocate and ultimately a leader in the Filipino-Australian community and in multicultural media.

When I was invited by the publisher of *The Philippine Times*, Alice Nicolas, to take over as editor-in-chief, I accepted the role wholeheartedly. Alice knew of my active involvement in the Filipino-Australian community as well as my interest in promoting Filipino culture in Australia and considered me to be a good fit for the role. Initially I did have some doubts as I do not have a journalism background. However, Alice ensured to support me from the beginning. Having Alice as my mentor to guide and support me has been very important.

## LEADING BY EXAMPLE AND WELCOMING CHANGE

The role of editor-in-chief is not one that just follows the news and edits articles. In fact, for me, it's a leadership role that captures a snapshot of the important happenings in the community and helps connect, promote and celebrate our diverse culture through various platforms, including our monthly print edition, as well as our digital presence via philtimes.com.au, our Facebook and Instagram pages, @philtimes. And with that, I support a small editorial and production team, as well as volunteer writers around Australia and in the Philippines. In order to meet deadlines and navigate both the planned and the unplanned that need due focus, I ensure the team is regularly informed and updated. I've helped steer the ship through difficult waters. Just over six months after I started, the COVID-19 pandemic began. There were no longer events to attend, and our publication was losing advertisers which actually led others in our team to start thinking about shutting the newspaper down completely.

Our team noticed that other community newspapers were no longer surviving, in an industry that was already in decline pre-pandemic. Deep down, I knew that our publication was different, and that we had the strength of our community to support us. I was noticing that the community needed us more during the lockdowns. I was truly caught by surprise as my role as editor-in-chief grew bigger with the increased demand for coverage.

With my vision to remain relevant to the community despite the uncertain times, I welcomed change. I helped keep the team inspired by providing them with updates of our good progress. I noticed that our social media engagement was increasing significantly and that our articles and other posts had higher engagements than we would normally see. Our work was recognised by community leaders and members (our readership), and our team was constantly encouraged and inspired to continue to do more.

In communication with my team, I ensure I am honest and responsive. Collaboration within the team became the norm. Working together with my team, I also lead by example by investigating new ways to capture stories and report them in a timely way via our website and social media. During the challenging and uncertain times, I was determined to lead the team to source stories of interest through our networks that mainstream newspapers such as *Herald Sun* began contacting me for! As society moved their primary communications online via social media during the pandemic, I ensured we made the most of these changes by using the platform to build our presence as a place where people come to access reliable, up-to-date news and information. Whatever was trending, I ensured we were covering and reporting in a timely way. This includes being quick to summarise and report the COVID-19 updates that were televised live on TV and social media. In other instances, I was featuring new Filipino businesses, including award-winning restaurant, Serai. Our impact was increasing as our stories inspired others to open their own small business. I was also proud that media, including in the Philippines were catching our stories too for their audiences.

As editor-in-chief, I supported the team through the times of survival and empowered them to stay optimistic and follow my approach of pivoting where possible. Being open to change ensured we were adaptable and set us up for our continued growth.

## WHERE PERSISTENCE AND DETERMINATION CAN TAKE YOU

Running a news platform on social media and producing a monthly newspaper is hard work. It's dynamic and at times unpredictable. My leadership role requires good organisation skills and a lot of focus as I liaise with multiple writers and sometimes advertisers throughout any given week of the month. There is not a day where I don't get contacted via phone, text, email or Messenger with a request for coverage or an invitation to an event. Nowadays, there are increasing demands for comprehensive coverage, including before, during and after an event for both print and on social media. There are sometimes also requests for me to attend meetings and small private events, as well as events interstate.

Unfortunately it does mean that I have many late nights throughout the year to meet strict deadlines with our printer. It's also a lot of Friday and Saturday nights at events, after working a full day. There was one time where I drove from Melbourne to Wagga Wagga in New South Wales, then back to Melbourne in one day! I reflect back on these moments and think about why I took on these engagements. And I realise that clearly, it's the passion I have for supporting the community. I lead by example, and I show others that I am genuinely interested and want to help their cause. Where a sincere invitation is extended to me, I always try my best to be present. And as a leader, I ensure I express my gratitude in person and engage with those that share their appreciation for my support.

I'm so proud of what the team and I have achieved in these four years since I started. I led the team to help us build our social media presence from ten thousand followers when I began to now over eighty thousand followers on Facebook. I was able to interview the Premier of Victoria, Daniel Andrews, in July 2022. In October-December 2022, the team worked together on a new video project, highlighting the resilience of members of the community. Another highlight for me as editor-in-chief was attending the State of the Nation Address as a guest in July 2023, despite the short notice, the Office of the President arranged an invitation for me, as they value our role with the Filipino community in Australia. I've ensured we have a holistic approach to support and engage in a range of campaigns, from tourism, health, sport and theatre, which has led to engagements with Cebu Pacific, Philippine Women's Basketball Team and Miss Saigon Australia this year.

It certainly has been a year of recognition. In May 2023 I accepted the Advocacy of the Year Award 2023 for our team, from the TaxSmart Cafe Best of the Best Awards. *The Philippine Times* was also one of three special awardees at the 125th Philippine Independence Day Gala this year. Each award we receive is a confirmation to me that I am on the right track. For me personally, I was happy to know that people, including our Philippine Consul General and Philippine Ambassador highly value the work we do. And I truly consider each invitation to an event or to support a campaign as a special opportunity to connect and engage, as well as celebrate and grow.

## FROM CURIOSITY TO CULTURAL IMMERSION

In my teenage years, I was living with my mum and sister, and kept close touch with my Filipino nanny. My late Nanay (mother) Paz was really like an older mother or grandma to me. I truly believe that she helped to plant the seed of curiosity in my life, and she probably did so without realising it. The time I spent in my teenage years was not so much with school friends, but more so with my Nanay Paz. She'd speak to me in Filipino, often forgetting that I couldn't fully understand. I felt bad to tell her to translate, so I made an effort to follow with the key words – and just listened. I watched quite a few Filipino films, listened to Filipino music and continued to feel a yearning to learn more about Filipino culture. After I finished high school, I began to feel a big gap in my life. I was no longer 'busy' attending classes and submitting assignments. Therefore, I found myself helping a close friend who joined a Filipino community beauty pageant. And that's where my involvement in the Filipino community began. I was happy to follow where life was taking me by having an open mind, curiosity and an eagerness to learn more.

This growth mindset helped me fill the gaps in my life, and immersing myself in the community helped build on my passion and approach to future opportunities.

Starting from the bottom and enjoying endless volunteer opportunities

I began working in my local library at the age of fifteen, and I'm proud to share that my first ever job was as a shelver in a public library. Stacking shelves with books was something I'd do after school, three days per week. What it did for me was introduce me to the world of information through books. My mind was eager to learn and discover how I can help others.

In those days, I was still trying to figure out exactly what I wanted to do – I was young and eager to learn and become independent, and I knew I just really wanted to help others. I initially wanted to become a teacher, and even completed the first year of an undergrad course in education. However, being surrounded by people with similar values helped me realise that I enjoyed working in libraries much more. This led to me undertaking my librarianship degree at RMIT where I was recognised for my achievements with an encouragement award and rewarded with a casual job at the university. However, I was eager to do more. I wanted to feel that I was making a real difference to others. And I knew I was happy to surround myself with the community that I wanted to learn more about.

Volunteerism helped me gain experiences in different settings. In some roles I had very little training, so I ensured I approached all of the opportunities I had as a challenge. Since completing high school, I've been a reader at Filipino mass, an emcee at a beauty pageant, stage manager at a community play and several community festivals, as well as stage crew for several concerts. I even coordinated over one hundred separate acts and performers over two days for the largest Filipino festival in Melbourne. All of these experiences helped me grow and reaffirmed my desire to participate and contribute to society. The experiences challenged me to go out of my comfort zone and helped me to learn more about myself and how I engage with others.

As I approached my thirties and while working in libraries, I continued to volunteer in various roles. For three years I was the secretary of Share Me A Dream, a registered charity where I was able to support the development of a classroom as well as medical missions in disadvantaged communities in the Philippines. Both privately and through the charity, I donated thousands of books to libraries in the Philippines to help promote and support education for disadvantaged communities. At this time, I was also writing articles for *The Philippine Times*. I found joy being a part of different teams and working with different people to achieve a goal, and to lead and to share information.

Serving the community in whatever way I could helped me to grow to become the leader I am today, and I discovered I could do this best by sharing important information to others in the form of news and stories through written articles, and other forms such as images and videos.

## THE IMPORTANCE OF SELF-CARE AND WORK-LIFE BALANCE

As a person with a role which is important to a large community, I've certainly experienced my fair share of challenges and disappointments. The journey of learning, growing and helping others can be exhausting if you don't look after yourself.

Being of service to the community in my various capacities over the years as a volunteer while also working has led to burnout on a few occasions. As a person who is seen to be helpful, reliable and calm, I'm often the receiver of multiple invitations and requests. This leads to an immense sense of pressure to be prepared and be present at events which occur at the same time. As fun as the engagements can be, over time, it does get exhausting.

The experience of burnout manifested in various ways for me, especially migraines and insomnia. Therefore, self-care is an important term that I keep at the forefront of my mind in all my decision-making. And it's equally important to note that self-care is different for everybody.

Since my undergrad days, travel overseas and interstate has helped me reflect and recharge so I can be ready to return to what I'm passionate about. Travel became a way of helping me discover more about my culture, about myself and my identity. These trips helped me also to 'reset' and have a clear mind – a break from the 'rat race'. It's important to stay calm and level-headed as a leader, and this is something I am known for.

Travel also helped me feel comfortable in my own shoes, giving me an opportunity to build my resilience and confidence, and gave me a great sense of appreciation of my life in Australia. I met many people from different walks of life and developed some close friendships in the process and came back stronger and wiser than before. As costly as these travel experiences were at times, they all provided invaluable firsthand experiences that I would not have learned in a classroom setting. Therefore, I see travel as a form of therapy, but also an important vehicle for growth as an individual and as a leader.

## BE REAL, BE YOU

My advice to aspiring visionary leaders is to be yourself and be authentic. As a leader, I've found that staying true to yourself, being vulnerable and open to learn at any stage of my career is the key to success. I believe that reflecting on your core values and reconnecting with your roots is what will help you to become a good leader.

Ensure you have time to reflect and make the time to share your gratitude. I've come to notice that the most well-respected leaders in business and politics are those who are down to earth, who listen and are selfless. This will be easy for some to follow, but others will struggle.

It's also important to put yourself out there and try different things. If an opportunity presents itself and you are open and able to take it on, it's probably worth giving it a try. It is a risk worth taking if you want to become a leader in your field.

## IN A NUTSHELL

As a quiet, introverted teenager where I was purely stacking shelves, I did not clearly see a future where I would be in a leadership role. At the time, I lacked confidence and was unsure about my identity and purpose in life.

It is through the immersive experiences I had through volunteering, my appreciation for my mixed Filipino, Italian and Australian cultural heritage, my openness to learn and grow, my willingness to go outside my comfort zone to try new things which led me to where I am today.

Having this growth mindset is a gift that I'm fortunate to have. By leading with honest and responsive communication, having a collaborative spirit and staying optimistic has a positive flow-on effect on those I engage with on a daily basis. Creating a plan and setting goals is an important part of this process.

Through the support of family, friends, mentors and the network of people in the community that I've met on this journey, I am able to remain resilient and focused on my passion to serve, connect and support others to be recognised and celebrate our culture.

# ABOUT JASON

JASON CORDI IS THE editor-in-chief of Australia's longest-serving Filipino newspaper, *The Philippine Times*. He is the son of Filipino and Italian migrants and has a deep appreciation for a diverse range of migrant stories and experiences.

He was born and raised in Melbourne and discovered his passion for serving the community through the various roles he has undertaken. For over fifteen years, he has actively volunteered in community events, as well as three years as secretary of a Filipino-Australian charity.

Since completing a bachelor of business (information and knowledge management) at RMIT ten years ago, he has worked as a librarian in both academic and public libraries.

Jason stays connected with his roots, immersing himself in culture through food, language and travel. He enjoys discovering more about the culture and has visited the Philippines over fiftytimes.

Jason began his challenging yet rewarding community leadership role as editor-in-chief four years ago. Despite the impacts of COVID-19, production of the thirty-three-year-old publication has remained steady, and its social media following has increased substantially. Through his direct and active engagement with the community, he has helped the newspaper grow in recognition, which has led to innovative projects and new partnerships.

# AHMET KESKIN
# BEING CONSIDERATE

*An important ingredient for any individual, let alone someone in a leadership role is to be highly considerate of other people's needs and to then engage appropriately, taking into consideration their situation. It adds to your respectability and builds trust.*

WHAT MAKES A PERSON an *exemplary leader?* There are many definitions of leadership or what it means to be a leader. I believe it is important to be authentic and see *ourselves* as the leader we are or aspire to be. My journey in discovering my leadership style has been fluid. It has been developed by my passion for continuing to grow and learn, with a focus on being a genuine and considerate person – a person who values diversity, inclusivity, respect and resilience.

First and foremost, I define myself today as an Australian. That wasn't my definition during my identity discovery period as it changed from one definition to another. My family arrived in Sydney in the early seventies when I was just six months old. My first few years of school were spent at Bourke Street Public School in Surrey Hills. At the time, it was a hub of multicultural students with a variety of backgrounds. My year three class had a strong Greek contingent, along with people from Spain and South America. We had some Pacific Islander people as well, so it really was quite an eclectic classroom. I vividly remember being one of three students of Turkish descent in the classroom. When our family moved to Cabramatta in the western suburbs of Sydney, I found it to be vibrant community with people from Turkey, Greece, Italy and Yugoslavia – as it was known then.

By the time I was in my last year at high school, if you'd have asked me about my identity definition, I would have emphatically said I was Turkish – not including the word 'Muslim', just Turkish. I was a Turkish individual who practised the basic rituals as my faith was formed from basically hearsay from my parents. It was more about following through the practises and rituals because your family was doing it even if some of your Turkish friends were lapsed Muslims. I'd follow my parents' lead.

My spiritual awakening went hand in hand with my community activism as soon as I graduated from high school. I started attending religious discourse, where I'd listen to an Imam speak, learning what my faith was about. I'd listen to the stories from our Prophet's time, and that fuelled my enthusiasm to start being more active in serving the community. I feel it's important to mention here that in Islamic teaching, a Muslim's primary objective in life is to seek their Creator's pleasure. This is the driver for my and many Muslims' community activism. By reading our Prophet's life story I learnt that leadership requires you to be a practitioner first before you can inspire others to follow.

I noticed there were Muslim student associations at many other universities, but not at the University of Technology Sydney, where I studied telecommunications engineering. I decided I should start a Muslim student association to facilitate a place to pray, to have gatherings and use as a hub for others to meet and see there are other Muslims in the university. This was my first effort in doing something positive for the community – being an agent to create an environment for others who identified with their faith, which allowed for the transaction of experiences and camaraderie.

During those formative years, I also became something of an informal mentor and tutor. While completing year eleven and twelve, I had benefited from free tutoring at the mosque, provided by a person who volunteered his time to help. I was very grateful for his service and inspired to do the same, thus I too tutored, supported and guided students from years nine to twelve, not just with their studies, but by being an ear to listen and support them to overcome their anxieties. I was able to advise them that life is more than a final exam and there are many pathways and choices you could make to realise your purpose and potential. I gave them words of comfort and encouraged them to do their best. As I was the beneficiary of someone's time and knowledge, I felt it was important to give back and impart my learnings so they could steer through some tricky situations. I learnt to do this without any expectation of monetary reward for my time.

After graduating, I was still involved in helping support youth in the community. I was involved in an organisation that established a school. This new venture enhanced my vision along with my capacity to do things. I found the education field to be the ideal way to synthesise some of some of my values – respect, honour, consideration and trust so that the people I work with made every effort to be mindful in activating these values in their everyday conduction. I know I was not perfect, nor were the people around me, but our collective behaviour exhibited traits of ideal human characters. We wanted the school to cultivate virtuous and informed students who were connected with the community who strived to make their environment better through collaboration with others, who were respectful towards others and their opinions.

Learning from our experience in creating the school, we realised there was an opportunity to build relations between our community and the wider society. In 2000, a couple of us with engineering backgrounds came together and formally established the *Affinity Intercultural Foundation*. The purpose of the organisation was to engage in dialogue with a view of listening with respect, a commitment to learning about our similarities and differences so we enhance our understanding of the diverse society we live in. Our very first program was the inaugural Mosque 'open day' on 3 September 2001, a week before the tragic 9/11. This happened in Auburn Gallipoli Mosque in Sydney.

It was during this period I grew as an individual, a community member and professionally because 9/11 thrust the Muslim community into the spotlight and I along with others had to be effective communicators with important and clever messaging. Not to say we were trying to beguile anyone with our message but rather point out that there will be individuals in every community who think differently and act against the law. These people need to be treated in isolation and not be reflective of the community. We reached out to wider society with interfaith and intercultural activities, bridging the gap and explaining to people that *we are just like everyone else* who wants what's best for our children; one that's respectful and inclusive, seeking to better understand ourselves and the environment we live in.

When it was my turn to step into the CEO role, I was completely out of my depth, but it was the impetus I needed to grow as a leader. As a person who is by nature an introvert, I was stepping into circles where I had to engage with a diverse range of people. I was attending seminars at universities and think tanks. I realised I needed to bring myself up to speed and open my mind to new learnings and opportunities. I needed to change the way I think and realise that not everything has to come to an end point or conclusion but rather move the conversation forward.

My working career, particularly as a project manager, gave me exposure to a diverse range of skilled people so I was able to observe how they thought and acted. Being exposed to the DISC model during my working life allowed me to treat every individual with the due attention they deserved. Knowing how a person behaves puts you in good stead to know how to deal with that person and get the best outcome for both you and them.

When my family and I moved to Melbourne at the end of 2014, I saw an opportunity to augment my skills and establish new friends and opportunities. There is a different vibe in Melbourne where people are conducive to rally around a good cause. It's great to see that programs like Ramadan Iftar dinner programs where we 'break bread together', brings a wide sector of society together to share space and time together where they would otherwise not be able to do so. Setting up auspicious programs seem to attract people's curiosity which brings people from different professions and status together, who in most cases would not be in each other's company. For example, in 2023 we held the inaugural Shabbat – Iftar dinner with our Jewish friends at the ARK centre. The attendees were predominately Muslim and Jewish people who shared a sacred time together to observe each other's faith practice. In a world where divisive discourse is growing, we were able to bring the human interaction to the fore so that conversations yielded more similarities than differences. I believe this is the strength of the organisation, and I, as a member of this organisation, to provide safe spaces for interactions to take place. The mere fact we're attempting this in this era where people are easily slotted into camps is the challenge for people like me who are out there to bring others into the conversation.

I'm very fortunate to have the support of sincere people who chip in to help make things happen, as they have full-time jobs. We are lucky that most of the team are passionate about what we are doing and see it more as a life project – an objective to reach as many people as possible and take them on the journey with us. It's a journey of self-discovery, seeking understanding and offering respect and valuing everyone's presence. I believe these are the fundamental pillars of a cohesive and resilient society. It's great working with people who share this passion and what I need to do is to ensure everyone's voice is heard, their ideas are respected and be challenged so that we grow individually and collectively. Leadership is about steering the ship in the right direction with everyone's commitment and buy-in to the objective. Not everyone agrees about everything but when you have a committed majority you make progress.

It's inspiring for me, particularly in my interfaith and intercultural line of work, that I've met so many people who are genuine, authentic and sincere. Seeing those people in action, in their modesty and humility, is what keeps me motivated on my life project. It's what spurs me on and keeps me excited, but also keeps me grounded at the same time. I'm inspired when I get to see a person's maturity and completeness by how considerate they are as that is what I look out for. Most of the time people look for markers they rank highly in themselves and when they see it mirrored or exhibited in others, a natural affinity occurs between them. This is true for other traits as well. However, you should also keep an open mind and be ready to be challenged so that your growth is intrinsic and expansive. This allows you to be the well-rounded individual you seek to be. That's why I now identify myself as an Australian – an Australian Muslim of Turkish background as a conversation starter.

I've also realised that respect is the fundamental principle of every engagement I'm involved in. I've learnt to have an open mind; an attitude that you can 'learn from anyone', regardless of their status, education, ability or not, faith or position in the community. This will ultimately help you to become a better leader. There's a Turkish saying which loosely translates to: 'Knowledge is at the beholder of the person, not necessarily determined by the age of the person.' This means a person who's my junior in age, life experience, knowledge etc. can have a profound effect on my thinking. I've learnt to become a sponge, someone who takes in knowledge from everywhere and everyone.

My ongoing passion for my work is fuelled by a quest for knowledge and self-renewal, along with maintaining a healthy mind, body and spirit. Patience is another virtue I'm working on. It's a marker of a strong and passionate leader. Not all projects or ideas come to fruition in the predetermined time. Everything will bloom in their own time, so sometimes you can revisit an old project with a fresh approach when the inputs or situation has changed.

I'm a great believer on working on a project with an eclectic group. I find that diversity yields more ideas. You can feed off others' enthusiasm and become more agile and flexible in your thinking. There is no wrong answer or wrong contribution. Everyone's ideas are considered and carefully regarded. This, of course, can lead to vigorous debates which can sometimes lead us to respectfully disagree, but every opinion is considered. That mindset plays a big part in the role of a leader as you being approachable is what others around are looking for. Being approachable and listened to are essential requirements for someone who's at the front.

A story that resonates powerfully with me is the idea of seamless intervention. There was once a commercial on TV, endorsed by the Victorian government, where a young lady was travelling on public transport and a guy sitting opposite her was staring intently. A man noticed how uncomfortable the woman was becoming and actively stepped forward to the block the line of sight. That simple gesture showed the woman she was supported, and her discomfort was lessened. That's what we're trying to do around religious hatred. It's the simple gestures that can mean so much. If adversarial parties were to come together with the intent of listening to each other with respect, where they value that person for who they are and give them their due courtesy, I believe on more occasions those parties will leave with changed attitudes. They may even want to have a follow-up conversation to realise there is more similarities in their journey.

In terms of my leadership role and the legacy I would like to leave, well, I just want to be seen as a genuine, sincere and committed contributor to this great conversation called diversity and inclusion. If I'm remembered in that way, that's good enough for me. I certainly don't have all the answers to all the problems in our society, but collectively, through a wide range of responses we can work through the issues one at a time. I think it's very important to be a valued member of that process. It's not about me or the individual who stands up and makes all the speeches or takes all the accolades on behalf of an organisation, it's about the collective entity and their contribution.

With that in mind, the three things I'd like to share for aspiring leaders and leaders continuing to grow, are:

Be present in the moment – This is something I'm still working on and advice I would love to have given to my younger self. This suggests we focus wholeheartedly on the one thing we are doing *in the moment*. If you are listening to someone talk, give them your undivided attention. If you are working on a task, give it your best.

Be authentic – Be yourself. Be genuine. Do not try to disguise who you truly are. Don't make concessions. Be proud of yourself, your heritage, culture and your traditions. Recognise that you are not a complete project and that you have shortcomings but be determined to improve.

Be considerate – Be mindful of another person's needs and exhibit genuine empathy. Be aware of their body language and learn to understand when you have triggered them or they moved to a position of discomfort. Know when and how to engage to make others feel comfortable around you. I rate this virtue highly because I believe you become a better, well-rounded individual.

In conclusion, it's important to remember that no-one is perfect, no-one is a finished product. If we take the attitude we are a work in progress from cradle to grave, and keep an open mind to learn from each other, I think it will help us be better human beings. For me, it's about being a good human being above anything else.

There are many definitions for a leader, but no 'one' definition encapsulates everything I want to say about this topic. All I can do is continue to work towards being the best version of myself, by listening, learning and developing myself to be a caring and considerate person, perhaps tinkering in altruism. We all face a variety of challenges in our lives, but a good leader will respond to those challenges by taking into consideration all the factors involved, be open to feedback and opinions from others whether that turns out to be relevant or not. Sometimes, we may even need to ask for feedback.

Now, with over twenty years of being recognised as a leader in this interfaith and intercultural work, my aspirations are the same today as they were back then — to realise my potential as a human being and be a cog in the wheel that works to build a respectful and resilient society, which is proud of its diversity and inclusivity. Our society will be stronger when we can work through issues together and benefit from everyone's perspective and input.

## ABOUT AHMET

AHMET IS THE EXECUTIVE director of the Australian Intercultural Society. He is one of the co-founders of Affinity Intercultural Foundation and was a NSW Centenary ANZAC ambassador. He was a recipient of the Western Sydney University (formerly UWS) Community Service Award 2013. He also started the UTS MSA where he studied bachelor of telecommunications engineering. He completed his master's in Islamic sciences with Islamic Sciences & Research Academy Australia through Charles Sturt University. He has been actively involved in community activism for over twenty-five years, with the last eighteen years in the area of intercultural dialogue.

# RIK SCHNABEL

# A MIND SET TO MILLIONS

*The questions you might be asking yourself right now could be, Are my thoughts becoming things? Is the sum of my life, the collection of all my thoughts? Is my income capped by my beliefs? Truer words could not be spoken.*

THREE PHONE CALLS HAD me earn more than Australia's prime minister. My wealth mindset came from three transformational phone calls. It is what I now teach people from all over the world. I am passionate about helping people get beyond their limits. But I had to learn a key lesson first. I promise you, that when you get this, your life will never be the same.

Melbourne winters can be cold. Wear as many clothes as you want, but when those icy winds blow fiercely you may as well be naked. But on one of Melbourne's worst freezing winter days, I couldn't feel a thing. I felt nothing but the weight on my shoulders. The realisation of my grim situation sunk in. I was just married with my first child and life was more expensive than my income could bear. I had more month than money. Twenty-seven dollars was all that I had to my name.

In the shadows of my mind, I could hear David Byrne singing that line from 'Once in a Lifetime', that Talking Heads song, 'How did I get here? Where is my beautiful house …?'

It's strange, what you can remember from your lowest of lows. Like a persona non grata with a raincloud following above me, I walked among the city streets to my office job. I worked in the Rialto building on Collins

Street, Melbourne, on the forty-sixth floor. Along the way, I got lost in my thoughts, feeling sorry for myself. I figured based on my income versus my bills, that the streets that I walked along would soon become my home. Being homeless wasn't the life I saw in my future, yet here I was.

*How did I get here?* It wasn't because I lost a job or made silly investment decisions. In fact, my lack of money all came down to accepting a job. A sales job in radio advertising. A job I couldn't do. Though this led to a kundalini awakening that moved up my body and changed my perspective. This epiphany changed my life forever.

But let me go back to what I thought was the cause of my problem. The decision to take a commission-only sales job was not the problem. Another decision gazumped me. The ludicrous decision I made, that had me believing that I was the worst salesperson I'd ever known. My poor position was the result of all my thinking.

On this day, I was about to learn that life can pivot in a second if you let it. If you believe it.

Up until this point in my life, I never believed in myself. I never believed that one powerful belief held the power to transport you out of hell and into heaven. Let me take you to the day that everything changed for the better.

I came off the street and I walked into the foyer of the Rialto Tower and took the lift to my office on the forty-sixth floor. Ironically, here I was with $27 in my bank account and working in one of Melbourne's iconic symbols of success with a poor, lowly attitude. Before I walked into my office, I hesitated and stopped at the door. I recalled the words of a mentor. A crazy American trainer with some illogical beliefs that served him well.

He once told me that before he was a millionaire, he was homeless. He said his belief in himself made him millions. Not his investments. Not his years of blood, sweat and tears. His beliefs saved him.

My American mentor said he got busy on changing his beliefs and now he made millions in a weekend. I knew this. I saw him do just that. He told me that the key understanding is, 'Thoughts create things, and with the right thoughts, anything is possible.'

All my issues became palpable. It became so obvious; I could now see that my thoughts had created the path to my financial ruin.

At my office door, I metaphorically drew a line. I decided that from this point I would create a new reality. New thoughts to create new things. I decided to pretend I was a multimillionaire. I imagined what my life would be like if I had $13 million dollars in my bank account. I don't know why I chose $13 million; it was the first number that popped into my head, and I felt a huge calm run through my body. I opened the door to my office and imagined I was walking into the epicentre of creation. This is where my wealth was to begin.

I walked to the back of my office. Up to the floor-to-ceiling glass and imagined all the people that I was helping. There had to be many appreciative clients, right? Otherwise, where would my millions come from? A smile came across my face and made me realise how long it had been since I smiled.

It was then that I heard a voice in my head that said, *You are the source of wealth, not your clients.* Perhaps these were words that came from a book I read or from my mentor? I just knew these words were true.

I imagined what it felt like to have millions in my bank account. Akin to proselytising, I could feel my beliefs that led to my low self-esteem and inept sales skills evaporate from me. All my stress, fear and worry melted away. In my imagination, I could see, hear, smell, taste and feel like a calm multimillionaire would. Then something happened that changed my life forever.

I guess I had induced a state of self-trance because my fortune became conceivable and felt believable.

My office phone rang and immediately brought me back to work.

I picked up the receiver. The caller on the other end of the phone proceeded to place an order that earned me half a year's income in commissions.

After I took the order and hung up the phone, the air around me was electric. I was in shock.

My mind buzzed between the contrasts of the day. I could feel it switching, trying to make sense of it all. Something inside of me knew that a miracle had occurred.

All my financial concerns and my fear of homelessness disintegrated. You could be forgiven for thinking that one phone call did all of this. It was something else. Something much more profound.

You see, before this moment, for eight months my phone hardly rung. Other than phone calls from my wife, friends and my sales director, my phone only rang one other time. About a month ago it rang with news of a paltry order for $3,500 for some advertising.

Rising to my feet with renewed belief and vigour, I again went up against the window of my office. I recalled my process prior to the previous phone call. Conditioning my imagination, soon I could see, hear, smell, taste and feel like a calm multimillionaire again. It was a blissful feeling. A deep sense of peace and contentment filled me.

The little hairs on the back of my neck shot up when my phone rang again.

Almost expecting a duplication of the previous call. I wasn't surprised when the next caller gave me an order that was similar in size to the order before it. Only this time, my commission was $1,000 more. Wildly appreciative, I did wonder if I had limited the amount I earned somehow. The two were so close in amount.

The excitement I held in my body lasted for days even though no more calls came to my office phone.

Then after three weeks had passed, I decided to walk up to my office window again.

Conditioning my imagination again to see, hear, smell, taste and feel like a calm multimillionaire. I felt a sense of apprehension; an expectation, if you will. This caused a tension. So, I said to myself, *It's okay, in two weeks you have created a whole year's income. Let it go.* It didn't matter even if I never got another sale that year.

With the pressure now eased, I imagined I was playing a wealthy character in a movie. I could see my reflection in the glass and thought, *If you're a multimillionaire, how do you earn all that money? Who do you serve and why do you care?* In that moment, I realised how much I cared for humanity. How much I truly wanted to help people. It was why I graduated as a life coach. It is the reason I continued my training in coaching, hypnotherapy and neurolinguistic programming. I didn't want to just help people; I wanted to transform their lives.

The phone rang again.

You could only imagine what I was thinking in that moment as I picked up the receiver. In that moment, I earned the sum of the first two amounts combined. In three weeks, I earned two years' salary. I knew something inside of me had changed forever.

In the next three months, I transformed from being the worst salesperson in the history of the company to becoming the best. I broke long-held sales records and my monthly income started to look like my annual income. I became the company's hero and the most celebrated sales star.

Though this led to my next career transition. I knew my mindset shifts were responsible for my success. I wasn't doing anything different. I was just thinking differently.

Soon, I realised that I loved helping people change their thinking and improve their lives. Why didn't I focus on this full-time? Improving their minds was more important to me than selling radio advertising. I knew then that it was time to leave my job and get on with my passion.

In 2004, I started my own company, *Life Beyond Limits*. Using what I learned in my sales transformation, I went on to make millions of dollars.

I coached, trained and sold self-development courses and resources.

The questions you might be asking yourself right now could be, *Are my thoughts becoming things? Is the sum of my life the collection of all my thoughts? Is my income capped by my beliefs?* Truer words could not be spoken.

The story I share with you today started in 2002. In 2004 I wrote a book about my transformation and shared my complete formula. The book, now called *A Richer Way to Think*, went on to become a bestseller and has helped many people see the world in a completely different way. It is how you see the world that determines how the world shows up for you.

## THE GREATEST LESSONS IN LIFE DO NOT COME FROM SCHOOL

What I have come to learn is that, ironically, nowhere in my entire education was I ever taught to learn. No memory techniques or retention strategies were shared. My teachers lectured, questioned and tested but never gave me systems of thinking. Not once were my beliefs called into question. I was never encouraged, yet at times made to feel less and made to feel small.

My parents modelled a punitive system to ensure that I toed the line and never broke their rules. Other than their parents, no-one taught them to parent. No-one told them how damaging to one's beliefs demeaning name-calling can be. Nor did they know how one's self-belief plummets from being physically punished.

Our parenting and schooling are the cornerstones of our lives. As sociologist, Dr Morris Massey, attests, our first seven years become the rest of our lives. Our habits, values, beliefs and our identity determine all we can and can't do. They tell us what is possible and what is not. Unquestioned, we come to believe who we are and in time, why we are who we are.

## HOW DO WE CHANGE OUR MINDS – UNTRAIN OUR BRAIN?

A successful media personality once fell through a shop display at the front of a store. His embarrassment due to his ataxia from multiple sclerosis (MS). His MS caused his poor muscle control and gave him clumsy involuntary movements. His difficulty with walking and balance was a blow to his pride, so, he reached out to me for help.

I told him, 'I've never worked with MS and wouldn't know the first thing to do.' He responded, 'I think you do. Just untrain my brain.' On his insistence, I agreed to work with him. We explored his belief systems and questioned his early decisions that he made about his physical limits. Frankly, I was making it all up as we went. In a few months, his symptoms of MS completely vanished. I was as surprised as he was. No more ataxia and he was completely in control of his life again. He was the man who gave me the title of 'brain untrainer'.

As a brain untrainer, most of my work in helping my clients to achieve is focused on untraining their brains. Shifting their beliefs. Clearing the trauma they endured, mostly, in those first seven years.

Often, I help executives and business owners, who may seem to be successful but suffer from imposter syndrome or a low self-esteem. Fame and fortune do not ease an undermining psychology.

I've helped rockstars and actors who use drugs and alcohol shut out or turn down those little critical voices in their heads. Mostly due to guilt they feel for the mismatch between fame and all they think they are not. Onstage and in front of the camera they cope by building a stage persona that carries off the facade. Out of the public eye, they fall into bouts of insecurity, depression and shame.

While 'thoughts create things', it is your past that has created your thoughts. Your past is nothing less than the sum of all your beliefs, values, patterns and decisions. This gives rise to understanding why at times the thing you want most stands defiantly in front of you, always out of reach.

Though if you are willing to be courageous. If you are willing to change. Anything is possible with the right guidance and some healthy brain untraining. You too could have a mind set to millions.

# ABOUT RIK

RIK SCHNABEL IS THE brain untrainer with over 38,000 brain untraining hours. He is a master of helping his clients create a life beyond limits and is a multiple bestselling author, a world-class master NLP trainer, a leading life coach and life coach trainer, a radio host and a passionate and articulate force for good in the world.

As a world leader in his field, he's been teaching life and business coaches since 2004 using the latest transformational tools. While most coaches use simple coaching models, Rik Schnabel uses neurolinguistic programming, EFT, cognitive behavioural therapy, time line, hypnosis, clean language, Mbit technologies as well as many techniques he's designed himself. He's the go-to when all else has failed.

# MARIA LOURDES SALCEDO
# EMBARKING ON A LEADER-SERVANT JOURNEY IN THE PHILIPPINE FOREIGN SERVICE

*If there is a common thread that binds my journey as a leader/public servant, it would have to be my passion for learning, not just for material knowledge but more importantly for key lessons in life. I search for it. I nurture it. And I like sharing it.*

IT WAS MEANT TO be a glossy start for the newly minted diplomat. But before I could flap my wings and fly, my director brought me back down to earth. 'Don't you think of yourself as special. Foreign service officers (FSO) are a dime a dozen. You are a servant first before you're a diplomat,' she quipped. Never mind that we use *dyes sentimos* not dime for ten cents. The statement surely drove home the message that it will not be an easy job.

I took the FSO exams (FSOE) in 1995. There were over two thousand who signed in for the qualifying exams, and in the final tally, there were forty-five or so of us left. After the first exams, there was a battery of written tests for three days covering topics such as Philippine history and government, world affairs and history, international economics, global trade and investment, diplomatic and consular practices, English, Filipino and foreign languages (I chose Nihongo). There were also interviews by several experts, group discussions, and of course, a psychological test. And then on to a six-month classroom training course and at least two years of on-the-job work experience before becoming eligible for an overseas assignment.

## IN SEARCH OF LEADERSHIP COMPETENCIES

Having passed the FSOE, I was expected to be a leader in the making ready to take on challenging roles to represent Philippine national interests. It took twenty-five years, however, before the Department of Foreign Affairs (DFA) institutionalised its competency framework with a department order signed in November 2020 to identify competencies required by the Philippine foreign service. By then, I was four years into the job as executive director of the DFA's Human Resources Management Office (HRMO).

The competency-based HRM is a commitment made by the DFA in its 2011-2016 Strategic Plan which is a response to the marching orders of the Civil Service Commission (CSC) to 'ensure that the development and retention of a competent and efficient workforce in the public service is a primary concern of the government'.

The task fell on my shoulders as I sat on my desk on my first day of work in November 2016 after my stint as Deputy Chief of Mission and Consul General in Yangon, Myanmar. I rummaged through the files of my predecessor to see what had been done to implement the commitment. Nothing much, it seemed, and the successor plan was due.

To be fair, I knew that there were other urgent tasks at HRMO on a daily basis: benefits and welfare of employees, rotation of personnel to eighty-eight foreign service posts (FSP) around the globe and thirty-seven consular offices around the country, training and scholarships, hiring and firing, and the list goes on. Not to lose sight, of course, is CSC's big picture of 'a continuing program of career and personnel development, merit promotion plans and performance evaluation system to be established for all government employees at all levels'.

My plate was not only full, it was overflowing. The assistant secretary was also assigned overseas a week or two after my assumption of office. All of a sudden, I was also the acting assistant secretary for HRMO, a very demanding task that required regular reporting to a very demanding undersecretary for administration. By then, I was conscious that I had to use a different part of my brain and tap on its connectors to help me become not only an efficient manager but also a good leader. Human resources work is not like that of policy analysis and advocacy which I was used to up to this time. With around 3,700 personnel who were expecting our 'leadership guidance', the task ahead was like scaling an unknown mountain.

Once the assistant secretary was appointed, I went back to getting the competency-based HRM off the ground, starting with my ten-day training at the Ateneo Center for Organizational Research and Development (CORD). In the ensuing months, the following were to be undertaken to implement the integrated competency-based HRM:

- Conduct an inventory of all designations and positions in the department and their corresponding job descriptions and competency profiles.
- Conduct a department-wide training needs analysis.
- Revise and implement training modules to address competency gaps of personnel.
- Embed competency requirements in the recruitment process.
- Institutionalise competency requirements in the placement/rotation of personnel to appropriate positions.
- Institutionalise competency requirements as one of the factors for promotion of personnel to the next rank.

After months of consultations and assessment reviews, the project was able to identify seven leadership competencies required of FSOs: (1) Strategic and critical thinking; (2) Institutional strengthening and innovation; (3) Partnering, networking, collaborating and consensus building; (4) Capability building; (5) People management; (6) Results orientation; and (7) Resource and information management.

The leadership competencies are on top of eight core competencies expected of everyone employed at the DFA: (1) Observance of duty to country and to DFA; (2) Ethical conduct, credibility and integrity; (3) Adaptability and resilience; (4) Efficient delivery of solutions and results; (5) Service orientation; (6) Effective communication; (7) Cultural and diplomatic sensitivity; and (8) Teamwork and collaboration. There were also dozens of technical competencies for specific designations.

Did I really possess all those fifteen or so competencies and demonstrate them not just sometimes, but always, and at a level worthy of a true leader, meaning at an advanced level? I sometimes wonder, but then I am not alone in this kind of introspection.

## JUNIOR OFFICER, JUNIOR LEADER

In January 1997, I entered the halls of the Department of Foreign Affairs, the first Philippine agency established in 1898 after the declaration of Philippine Independence, thinking, *I belong here.* At one end of the polished floor was the statue of the first Secretary of Foreign Affairs, Apolinario Mabini, the so-called 'brains of the Philippine Revolution' seated on a pedestal. To the left were the busts of those who served as his successors, with the title 'Secretary of Foreign Affairs'. It did not feel particularly intimidating to be sized up by these 'cream of the crop'.

Following my cadetship program, I was assigned as Principal Assistant to the Office of European Affairs. Nothing exceptional there except for piles upon piles of documents to review and letters to respond to such as, *Is it true that Filipinos eat dogs?* Or, *Would the first woman Philippine President want to marry a cosmetic surgeon so he can make her nose slimmer?*

Then one day in July 1998 I was told, along with another junior officer, that we were to accompany the new president to the Leaders' Summit of the Asia Europe Meeting or ASEM in London. The president was to be assisted or coached when to speak and what to say. I had devised colour-coded index cards for his talking points and these were checked and rechecked by my director, the executive director and the assistant secretary. The 'traffic lights' (green for volunteer to speak, yellow for speak when asked and red for do not speak) were ready when we were told that the president decided to delegate the senate president to attend on his behalf. As the senator was an excellent speaker, he did not need the 'traffic lights' for his talking cues.

## HARROWING BUT FULFILLING EXPERIENCE

Not long after my stint at the ASEM Leaders' Summit in London, a directive was issued for my transfer to the Office of the Undersecretary for Migrant Workers Affairs (OUMWA). I was to help set up a policy assessment and advocacy desk and handle controversial cases involving women migrant workers. The first part of the task was something I had always wanted to do but the other half, I must admit, was the most stressful experience.

As the special assistant to this office, I often went through all the reports concerning Filipino migrant workers from FSPs, mostly from the Middle East, with such harrowing stories as public beheading, seafarers getting involved in drug smuggling or domestic helpers jumping from windows of high-rise buildings. Once the head of the office (called Consular Assistance Division) went on leave at around the time when a Filipina married to an Indian in Singapore killed her three young children. She obviously lost her sanity which drove her to this most horrendous act. The detailed report was so vivid in my head for several days that every time I got to the gate of DFA, I heard a ringing in my ears and a slight pounding on my chest. That the media hunted me down for more information did not make it easier for a mother like me.

Behind those dreadful and heart-rending cases, however, is a source of possibilities. We managed to better understand the push and pull factors of migration, the phenomenon of feminisation of labour migration and even tested a framework of assistance for women migrant workers by empowering them to access help whenever needed. In the process, the media branded me *kasangga ng mga kababaihang manggagawang Pilipino* or partner of Filipino women migrant workers.

The position also gave me a chance to be a part of the public consultation in defining human trafficking based on the cases that we documented. The string of meetings led to the need to put together a legislation to address human trafficking. The bill was passed into law in 2003 when I was already assigned in Canberra.

## UNIO AND NON-ALIGNED MOVEMENT

The highlight of my assignment at the office of UN and International Organizations (UNIO) was the important role that my division took in making preparations for the Special Non-Aligned Movement (NAM) Ministerial Meeting on Interfaith Dialogue and Cooperation for Peace and Development held on 17-18 March 2010. Preceded by a preparatory Senior Officials' Meeting on 16 March, the SNAMM with 449 official delegates was the second biggest gathering in Manila of high-level government representatives in Philippine history, second only to the Ministerial Meeting of the United Nations Conference on Trade and Development (UNCTAD) in 1979. As a result, I received a presidential citation from President Gloria Macapagal-Arroyo. We also managed to publish a substantive and beautifully crafted book called *Peace Through Interfaith Dialogue: Philippine Diplomacy and the Promotion of Mutual Understanding, Respect and Tolerance.*

Earlier in July 2009, I was lucky to have been approved as a member of the Philippine delegation to the Fifteenth Conference of the NAM held in the Egyptian Red Sea resort of Sharm el-Sheik, lending support to President Arroyo, one of the fifty-five heads of state attending. Preparing for this meeting, I had to be in direct contact with the president's assistant at the palace for long hours on end until the day of the actual meeting when I was up close and personal with the Philippine president for the second time, right there in a country I have never imagined I would be able to visit.

The president was chosen to speak, for and on behalf of the Asian group, after Libyan President Muammar Gaddafi, representing the African group. The instruction was for the speakers to speak for five minutes only and from their seat around the huge horseshoe table arrangement. Gaddafi broke protocol by jumping the barrier onto the stage to speak at the podium for forty-five minutes. He surprised everyone, including the Philippine contingent who scrambled to find a platform for the next speaker. Luckily, there were telephone directories around for the president to be able to rise above the podium to speak for exactly five minutes. That definitely drew a rousing applause from the audience.

On the second day of the meeting, the president decided it was her chance to see the St Catherine Monastery overlooking Mt Sinai where the Israelites apparently camped with Moses on their way to the promised land when they escaped from Egypt. The other Philippine officers had to be with the President, of course, and I was asked to 'keep the Philippine seat warm', which I gladly obliged. At the meeting, the presidents of Panama and Peru, to my left and right, respectively, commented that the 'Philippine president has grown taller and younger'. Luckily, the task only entailed taking down notes of what were said by the NAM leaders.

## FIRST AND LONGEST POSTING DOWN UNDER

I embarked on my first foreign assignment as third secretary and vice-consul in Canberra in November 2000. Tagging along with me as a single mother were two young children and their eldest sister (there's five of them) when we got to the capital city of Australia close to five o'clock on a Sunday afternoon. To our surprise, the city was quiet, which prompted my daughter to comment, 'Are you sure this is a city?' Canberra at that time had a population of around 340,000, growing by about 1.5% yearly on the average to its 2023 level of 472,000.

As the most junior of the three officers, I was in charge of consular section and also supervised the embassy's community and cultural activities. *Pasko sa Canberra* was one project we introduced back in 2004. Gathering leaders of the Filipino community in the Australian Capital Territory, we managed to put together a Filipino extravaganza of music, food, crafts and Christmas revelry. Nineteen years later, it remains a distinctly Filipino festival awaited by Canberrans.

Australia is such a vast country for our mission to cover. I remember accompanying my Ambassador to the Northern Territory in 2003, not only to see the wild beauty of the top end but also to learn about unheralded linkages of our Filipino ancestry in the southern hemisphere. The Dean of Aboriginal Studies at Charles Darwin University toured us to a cemetery where we saw graves of many Filipino names. They were the so-called Manila men who worked as pearl divers of northern Australia at a time when there were no states nor territories yet. We also met some of the descendants of Filipinos who married indigenous women. They shared their versions of Filipino dishes such as *pansit, adobo, mechado, dinuguan* and other dishes.

Another trip took me to Tuvalu, also covered by the Embassy along with Nauru and Vanuatu. It is a country composed of three reef islands and six atolls in western Pacific. With a total land area of only twenty-six square kilometres, it is considered the fourth smallest country in the world. Halfway from Nandi to Funafuti, our pilot declared 'the plane is going back'. With instructions from the ambassador, I learned from the flight attendant that there was no-one in the airport and that the one on duty will be back from church after an hour.

As our plane landed on the runway also used to dry grains, one could see the sea on both sides of the Funafuti Atoll where the capital city is located. Trekking the small island, I saw a large colourful jeepney with a sign *Mabuhay*. It turned out to be brought home by an official who worked at the Manila headquarters of the Asian Development Bank. There were three Filipinos in Tuvalu: one was a doctor in the only hospital, another ran the only internet cafe and the third worked for an NGO.

At the lobby of our hotel, I heard local people speaking the Tuvaluan language and I could pick up a few words akin to major Philippine languages. I then asked the lady at the reception to count and lo and behold, half of the ten numbers are similar or sounding familiar. At the Tuvalu National Library, I read that Tuvaluans are Polynesians who share genetic affinity with those who also inhabited Southeast Asia some three thousand years ago.

A month or so before winding up my six-year tour in Canberra, I was requested to be extended for another seven months to help in the official visit of President Gloria Macapagal-Arroyo to Australia in May 2007. Both the political appointee ambassador and his deputy were relatively new in the job and I was to provide the needed 'institutional memory' and networks. Receiving the second woman Philippine president was Prime Minister John Howard who commented during the state dinner at the Government House that 'Australia and the Philippines enjoy a long-standing relationship, cooperating closely on counterterrorism and sharing strategic interests in regional peace and security'.

In a span of six years and seven months, I served under four Ambassadors in Canberra, two of them were women. Years later, sitting for the oral exams for the second level of promotions for FSOs, I was asked how I compared the men and women ambassadors. I heard myself saying the men were good; the women were great achievers'.

## THE SOUTH CHINA SEA ISSUE WHILE IN HANOI

My assignment in Hanoi was quite eventful. Seventeen months into my posting in April 2012, the Scarborough Shoal stand-off in the South China Sea happened, leading to the elevation of the controversial nine-dash line to the Arbitral Tribunal in The Hague in January 2013.

Scarborough or Panatag Shoal (*Bajo de Masinloc* based on a 1743 Velarde map), are two rocks in an atoll some 119 nautical miles east of Luzon, the largest island of the Philippines. The stand-off began after the attempted apprehension by the Philippine Navy of eight main-land Chinese fishing near the shoal. The BRP Gregorio del Pilar which undertook the inspection on board the fishing vessels discovered ille-gally collected corals, giant clams and live sharks. Tensions ensued after Chinese maritime surveillance ships blocked the Philippine vessel. Since Vietnam is also a country disputing China's nine-dash line, I took close interest in monitoring the matter as the deputy to the ambassador.

From my consultations with ASEAN counterparts, many com-mented that Philippine officials could have quietly approached Chinese officials instead of 'running to Uncle Sam'. And even when the visit of the Secretary of Foreign Affairs was previously arranged, a quick detour to Beijing could have averted the standoff, they said. The stand-off resulted in the defacing of many government websites, blocking of Philippine fruit exports, boycott from Chinese tourists, unilaterally declared fishing ban and *a fait accompli* control over the shoal.

Before leaving for Hanoi in November 2010, I had a chance to meet the Deputy of the Vietnamese Embassy in Manila who asked me how come the Philippines had not disputed China's official submission to the UN of its map with the nine-dash line. The response to my report was obtuse: Vietnam's joint submission with Malaysia of their extended continental shelf was an issue. It took three years later before an offi-cial response to the nine-dash line could be de-linked from that joint submission.

Sitting for a bilateral consultation in 2013, I was puzzled why we had to be mum about the arbitral proceedings filed against China in the Permanent Court of Arbitration (PCA) in The Hague. Moreover, when asked if there should be any documentation of the informal consultation, I proposed a one-liner statement that 'the nine-dash line does not have any legal basis', to which I received some dagger looks from the bosses. That would have been anticlimactic and pre-empting the PCA, I soon discovered.

Meanwhile, I joined a consultation for a multilateral initiative for the code of conduct in the South China Sea or COC between ASEAN (Association of Southeast Nations) and China eleven years after the ASEAN-China Declaration on Conduct of Parties in the South China Sea was signed by the parties. There was a commitment to finish it in two to three years. However, it took another four years to agree on a framework agreement and another year to adopt a single draft. Twenty years have passed and it seems the much-awaited COC is nowhere finished.

In the course of my stay in Hanoi, I have keenly observed how the host government was able to leverage on its comradeship with the big neighbour vis-à-vis its budding relations with the US (relations normalised only in 1995) and expanding ties with Russia, Japan, South Koreas, EU and Australia. Vietnam at that time was almost overtaking the Philippines in economic progress and perhaps I was reading too much from what was happening. In 2022, Vietnam has already overtaken the Philippines in terms of gross domestic product (GDP) at USD1.32 billion vs. USD1.17 billion for the Philippines.

## YANGON, ASEAN AND AUNG SAN SUU KYI

Leaving the overlapping claims in the disputed waters behind, I requested for a transfer to Yangon, a hardship post, in mid-2013. I pursued the cross-posting to learn more about the interesting history of Myanmar (formerly Burma) and to acquire experience in the 25th ASEAN Summit in Nay Pyi Taw in November 2014.

Officially called the Republic of the Union of Myanmar, it is the largest country in mainland Southeast Asia and shares borders with China, India, Thailand, Laos and Bangladesh. It is very rich in natural resources such as gems, oil, natural gas, teak timber and solar power potential. However, it has the lowest GDP per capita among 10 ASEAN countries at USD1,053 in 2022, according to the International Monetary Fund. Years of struggle from warring states were protracted through much of the history of the country until the Anglo-Burmese wars in 1825, the start of British colonial rule. Over a century later after the country's independence in 1948, Burma was in one of the longest running civil wars. Military rule took over from 1962 to 2015 and again from 2021 up to this writing.

When I arrived in Yangon, the country was in the midst of democratic reforms, including the release of pro-democratic leader and Nobel laureate Aung San Suu Kyi from house arrest (a total of fifteen years between 1989 and 2010), the creation of the National Human Rights Commission, amnesty of political prisoners, and relaxation of press censorship. The reforms led to Myanmar's chairmanship of ASEAN in 2014, which included the attendance of Philippine President Benigno Aquino III.

One of the foremost tasks I took was to make courtesy calls on officials in the new capital Nay Pyi Taw, an entirely planned city some 377km north of Yangon. Announced to the public in 2006 during the Armed Forces Day, involving over twelve thousand troops, the new city capital was built over ten years. Apparently, it has been an ancient tradition to move the capital around to avoid foreign invasions and local uprisings. The Parliament complex, where Aung San Suu Kyi went to work between 2012 and 2021, was a jaw-dropping thirty-one-building architectural display of teak timber and jade stones. Crossing over a moat is a quiet 'high-way' of around ten to twelve lanes, which could easily accommodate a jumbo plane.

I met Aung San Suu Kyi when she invited members of the diplomatic corps to a meeting at the Parliament in the lead up to the 2015 general elections which her party, the National League for Democracy, won 86% of the seats in the Parliament. She was already a parliamentarian then having won a 2012 by-election. The world rejoiced at the democratic reforms which catapulted her to the new position of state counsellor, but she soon earned criticism for defending, or turning a blind eye on, the military (predominantly Burmese and Buddhist like her), for their treatment of the Rohingyas in Rakhine State.

Being involved in the preparations for and the actual ASEAN Leaders' Summit was well and truly hectic but instructive. I travelled many times to Nay Pyi Taw to accompany visiting Philippine officials call on Myanmar officials. A further 168 km north-east is the awe-inspiring ancient capital called Bagan, a UNESCO-heritage site of around two thousand old stupas, temples and monasteries built between the ninth and thirteenth centuries.

One of the most memorable work I did was to put together a project called 'Passion for Fashion' in 2016 to celebrate the sixtieth anniversary of Philippines-Myanmar diplomatic relations. With the help of a group of Filipino and Burmese volunteers, we managed to stage a stellar fashion show-dinner at the most upscale hotel in Yangon, showing the designs of four visiting Filipino fashion designers who collaborate with six local designers. With zero budget at the start, we managed to raise a net of USD15,000, which we donated to the Yangon Children's Hospital.

## MELBOURNE, MY RETURN ENGAGEMENT WITH AUSTRALIA

Quo vadis DFA retirement system?

At the final planning session for 2017-2022 DFA Strategic Plan, I was asked to represent my office where I told my assistant secretary I wanted to introduce a new paragraph to the document. This pertains to Section 62 of Republic Act 7157 or the 1991 Foreign Service Act, pertaining to DFA's retirement system, or lack of it. The proposed paragraph is merely to remind ourselves that for the longest time – twenty-six years to be exact – we have yet to do something about this provision in the law. In fact, this provision has been sitting idly in the precursor of the said law, RA 708 of 1959. I was told that perhaps this is a 'lost cause' and that is why nothing has been done about it.

Not to be dissuaded, I convened and chaired an Inter-Office Consultation Committee on the DFA Retirement Bill. After seven months, we sent a clean draft bill to other offices for comments and visited other agencies with special retirement arrangements such as the Supreme Court. In March 2020, just as the world was waking up to the realities of the COVID-19 pandemic, the Secretary of Foreign Affairs endorsed the draft legislation to House of Representatives Speaker Alan Peter Cayetano and Senate Committee on Foreign Relations Chairperson Aquilino Pimentel.

As I was leaving for my foreign assignment in November 2020, I saw the draft legislations of the DFA Retirement System, now numbered, by both Houses of the Congress. But then again, everyone accepted that survival was the order of the day and everything was at a standstill for more than a year. When Congress resumed after the prolonged lockdowns, there were many other priorities to be attended to.

After all these years, I'm still hopeful that something positive can come out of it and that many can, in fact, benefit from the fruits of our labour.

## ABOUT MARIA

Maria Lourdes Monteagudo Salcedo joined the Philippine foreign service in 1997 after passing the foreign service officers' exams in 1995.

Her most challenging assignment at Department of Foreign Affairs (DFA) was as a special assistant to the undersecretary for migrant workers' affairs in 1998 to 2000 where she helped set up the policy assessment and advocacy desk and handled controversial cases involving women migrant workers.

She also considers her stint as executive director at the human resources management office between 2016-2020 as 'fulfilling' when she introduced some strategic projects such as the competency framework, online foreign assignment portal, transformative coaching, DFA Collective Negotiation Agreement and the DFA Retirement and Disability bill submitted to both the Senate and House of Representatives in 2019.

She also collaborated with former Ambassador Delia Domingo-Albert for the publication of the pioneering book *Women in Diplomacy: The Remarkable Ambassadors in the Philippine Foreign Service*.

Currently the Consul General of the Philippine Consulate General in Melbourne, her past foreign assignments were at the Philippine Embassies in Canberra, Hanoi and Yangon.

Maria or Odette has five grown-up children – all professionals in their own chosen fields, and nine grandchildren.

# IAN STEPHENS
# THE MAGIC OF THINKING BIG

*Every truly inspiring leader has set a bold vision that galvanises their team and requires everyone to tap into their better self.*

57, 29, 26 AND 2011. Pivotal numbers in my life.

Yesterday I turned fifty-seven. And so far, my journey as a speaker, trainer and author has taken me to twenty-nine countries over the course of twenty-six years. I don't say that to impress you, but to impress on you that I would be an absolute idiot not to notice some distinctions about what drives and sets visionary leaders apart. If one trait of brilliant leaders stands out, it can be summarised as 'thinking big, being bold, and persisting in the face of resistance'.

Now back to that number … 2011. This was the year Karina and I decided to make a bold move. We wanted a property a small group of senior leaders could live in when undertaking my executive leadership coaching program. The right property turned up and it included a purpose-built three-room day spa. Given Karina was originally from the day spa industry in and around Ballarat in Victoria and needed a new project to stretch her entrepreneurial streak, we sold our house in Castle Hill. We moved into our retreat property on the Tweed Coast and were gearing up to open a five-star day spa. It was a move that stretched us, taking up all of our savings to make happen.

We hit a little snag when the local council insisted that the car park would need expanding to cater for staff and visitors. The lowest quote

I got for the earth moving was $15,000. Ouch! We didn't have a spare $15,000, let alone the $5,000 needed to convert a spare room in the pool house to a ladies' change room/shower. That week, we just said a little prayer of gratitude and handed the problem over to the universe. It was time to get out of the way, to let go, and instead let GOD (grand organising designer … or 'source' as we refer to it) get into action.

The following Friday, whilst clearing the mailbox, I bumped into the guy doing some earth moving nextdoor. I told him about what we wanted to do with the car park, and he came and had a quick look. He was back knocking on my door within the hour saying he had spoken to his boss in Sydney. They had no work for him the next week and given all the equipment was already on-site next door, his boss said he would accept $5,000 cash to do the lot, and I could pay it off over two months. Amazing. But wait … there's more!

The following Monday an unexpected refund cheque arrived for $9,000 from the mortgage insurer of our previous home. Our financial planner had arranged this as part of paying out our previous mortgage when we moved from Sydney to the retreat on the Tweed Coast. We had no idea it was even in motion. Ta-da! The universe had delivered yet again, within days of us doing the manifesting work. This refund cheque financed both the ladies' change room renovation and the expanded car park.

There is magic in thinking big and trusting that the universe will have your back.

*'Are you in earnest? Then begin this minute, for boldness has power, and magic in it. Begin it! Now!'*
**Johann von Goethe**

The idea of opening a five-star day spa was bold, and we began it! Every leader I have worked with over the course of my career, and the best-of-the-best of those I have coached, had one thing in common … they formulated a bold vision and had the passion and drive to bust through the barriers the universe threw up to test their resolve. So, it was time for Karina and me to walk-the-talk of what we call the BOLVIS principle represented by the eagle.

Eagles are very *bol*d animals, forthright and determined in their actions. They are the biggest bird in the sky – it is the domain that they rule. They can soar to great heights and have the gift of exceptional *vis*ion. They can see both the bigger picture and the opportunities hidden from view, hence the term 'eagle eye'. The smallest of field mice don't escape their highly tuned sense of sight.

The eagle's spirit totem message encourages you to have a big, bold, compelling future. Dream big, or have a clear *vis*ion, if you like. Hence, we call the eagle BOLVIS. It is a summary of the two key words I always want you to remember – be *bold* and have a strong *vis*ion, or goal. BOLVIS.

Tomorrow's reality is as big or as small as we imagine it to be. The subconscious realm of our mind cannot tell fact from fantasy and is a goal-seeking device. Does it not follow therefore that we should think big?

David J Schwartz, in his classic book, *Thinking Magic of Big,* says …

*'Case history after case history proved that the size of one's bank account, the size of one's personal happiness, and the size of one's general satisfaction account, is determined by the size of one's thinking. There is magic in thinking BIG.'*

I do remember reading a book by Denis Waitley, *The New Dynamics of Goal Setting.* His mentor, the late Earl Nightingale, told the story about a farmer who came across an old glass jug in his pumpkin patch. As an experiment, he poked a very small, green pumpkin into it.

Months later, when the field was fully developed and about ready for harvest, the farmer again came across the glass jug. The other pumpkins on the same vine were large and fully developed, but the pumpkin in the jug had not been able to grow beyond the confines of the glass and was shaped to its exact dimensions!

I guess I need to ask, what kind of jug are you struggling to grow in? If you enlarge the size and the shape of your goals, and then create a detailed blueprint for achievement, your dreams can take any shape you care to give them. In other words, your success can be as big as you dare to envision it. You should think big, be bold and persist.

Persistence is yet another trait of the eagle. Eagles can make as many as fifteen attempted strikes before success is achieved. They don't give permission for anyone or anything to cause them to let go of what is right for them. They are very persistent in catching their prey … sometimes eventually. They teach us to not get stuck in 'analysis paralysis'. We must grab and maximise opportunities. Eagles also have extremely large and strong talons capable of holding onto prey of their own weight. This is symbolic of the ability to grab opportunities which materialise when we have an end in mind.

The eagle is a brilliant metaphor for being bold and chasing your goals and intentions. In all the years I have been working with companies creating high-performing teams, the BOLVIS principle has been there. Show me a team that is working well together, and I will show you one that has a collective bold vision of where they want to go and what they want to achieve. As the bible says, 'For the lack of a vision, people perish.' We love to be part of something that is bigger than ourselves. We love that sense of belonging achieved when we sign on to a team BOLVIS.

*'The greatest danger for most of us is not that our aim is too high and we miss it, but that it is too low and we reach it.'*
**Michelangelo**

Let's duck back to 1987 when I aimed low and reached it. Subiaco. Perth, Western Australia. I'm in a gym watching some guys mucking around on a speedball (referred to as a speed bag in the USA). You know the one that Rocky made famous – a small ball hanging down from a platform and one of the most difficult things in the world to control. These guys made it look easy. The rhythm was cathartic. It was talking to my soul. I did what most people do when trying the speedball for the first time; I waited until everyone else had gone home! I was the only one in the gym apart from the personal trainers who were busy and distracted cleaning up to close shop. I walked up and gave it a go. Well, to say I was pathetic is an understatement. The ball was out of control immediately and about a minute after trying it, I gave it a final heavy punch muttering out loud, 'Friggen stupid thing! Who the hell invented this?' I walked away and was plain out of the speedball game for the next decade. My aim was very low.

Can you relate? When was the last time you gave up on something too early because of fear, uncertainty or a lack of knowledge and skills?

Fast-forward to 1997. I have made the finals of the Speedball Freestyle event at the National Boxercise Championships in Melbourne. Six months earlier I had met Roger Anthony when I attended his 'Crocodiles not Waterlilies' *Self-Leadership Team Dynamics* program. At the back of the seminar room was a portable speedball unit he used as a metaphor around mastery. His father had taught him the dying art of freestyle speedball. He asked for volunteers who wanted some coaching on how to master the speedball. With my pathetic attempt a decade ago still fresh in my mind, I raised my hand and was soon receiving tips and knowledge. I joined forces with Roger and he soon became a mentor in business and life – *and* my speedball coach.

Back to the national championships … After only three months of tutoring by Roger, it's my turn. Three minutes to step up in front of a 500-strong audience and impress the judges with a routine that showcased my range of freestyle movements. I was so nervous. My mouth was dry. I was literally scared spitless!

I came second. Second to my coach and mentor. Not bad.

It was Roger who, months earlier, had inspired me to have the courage to chase my dream, resign from the certainty of my safe corporate job and fully step into being a full-time speaker, trainer and educator. After six months in my new career, I was living the dream facilitating some workshops, delivering the odd speaking keynote, enriching lives and … I was dead broke! Have you ever been there? Too much month at the end of the money? Money was very slow coming in the front door but was still going out the back door as fast as ever. The mortgage, a young growing family, the bills to be paid. They say money talks but all it said to me in those years was 'bye-bye'!

This was the first time in my life I was getting behind on my big-mouth promises. The credit card debts were mounting and my wife at the time was asking, 'What are we feeding the kids this weekend? The EFTPOS has declined … again!'

My first wife of ten years, Tamie, had always been very supportive of me chasing my dreams. And whilst we have always remained good friends in the spirit of co-raising our wonderful kids, have you ever noticed how financial pressure has the ability to magnify fine hairline cracks in a relationship? When a small vein of water gets into cracks in a rock and freezes, it can split a boulder in two. So too did our marriage break apart.

I was now living the four Ds. I was divorced, in debt, depressed and … de bank was chasing me. I had been king-hit by life. I was down on the canvas and my initial reaction was to curl up on the floor, adopt the fetal position and suck my thumb.

It was during this period that the lessons from the speedball training came back to me. My speedball started talking to me. Do you remember Tom Hanks' character in the movie *Castaway?* He developed a relationship with the volleyball he called Wilson. Well, my speedball became my Wilson. He didn't actually talk to me (crikey – send me off to the funny farm if that was the case!) but a voice inside my head started reminding me that I had to get up and keep punching. And for some strange reason, my Wilson's voice sounded like Rocky's coach in the first two movies, Mickey. *'Come on – you've got one more round in ya. It's not how hard you get hit. It how hard you come back from the hits. Remember the great Ali's advice that true champions are just prepared to always go one more round!'*

And so, I did. I got back up with renewed vigour and the awareness that I had to persist. A week later I was asked to fill in for a sick speaker at a huge industry event planning conference in Melbourne. The last thing I felt like doing was trying to inspire others when I just wanted to stay in bed, pull the covers over my head and hide from the world. But I designed a keynote, dragged my portable speedball unit down to the Exhibition Convention Centre, set up and waited for the audience to file into my breakout room session. Unbeknownst to me, the owners of the largest speaking bureau in the southern hemisphere, Saxton Speakers Bureau, were in the audience. At the conclusion, and after incorporating my three-minute speedball championship routine into the session, we struck up a conversation. This led to me working with their sales team, which led to them representing me exclusively for my speaking engagements and promoting me to their international client base. And so started a long and fruitful relationship for both parties. Nanette Moulton and the late Winston Broadbent became friends, business partners and confidantes. They would go on to book me for an average of thirty paid professional speaking engagements every year. Serendipity had intervened and created a defining moment in my life.

I will always be grateful for Nanette and Winston, and the inner guidance to just persist a little longer, trusting that the breakthroughs would happen.

It could have easily gone another way. During the darkest days of those times, I had even polished up my résumé and listed it with several recruitment agencies with the view to getting into a well-paid leadership role back in the insurance industry. I thank God for the quiet whisperings which kept me on track to stay the course.

## THE RETICULAR ACTIVATING SYSTEM

I am also grateful that our subconscious mind has a tool associated with it which acts like a homing device to home in on what you want. There have been numerous times in my life when the power of *getting a clear vision* has been reinforced. These occurrences always remind me that our mind has a *reticular activating system* (or RAS for short). The RAS is just like a filter system. The subconscious is bombarded with thousands of bits of information every minute, via all the body's senses. It therefore likes you to be very specific about what you want so it can screen out any thoughts or distractions that are not in alignment with your desired outcomes. As a result, you notice those things that are a good fit to your desires.

My first car was a small Gemini panel van. Don't laugh! It was the early 1980s (for the younger generations, you might have to google a 1979 Holden Gemini panel van to get the picture – literally!). A couple of years later I was promoted to the role of team supervisor, so I decided the Gemini was no longer cutting the image. I made the decision to upgrade to a metallic brown Mitsubishi Scorpion Coupe. (You're laughing again … grrr!) Having made the decision to buy a Scorpion, I suddenly noticed metallic brown Scorpions everywhere. Has this ever happened to you? The car you desire starts pulling up beside you at traffic lights, parks next to you in shopping centres and you see them parked in driveways as you drive home. For me, it was like Mitsubishi had suddenly flooded the Australian market with metallic brown Scorpion Coupes. THEY WERE EVERYWHERE. This was not the case, of course, but it felt that way to me. All that had happened was I had given my subconscious mind a series of specific instructions on the exact car I wanted. I was able to filter out all other vehicle types. Three weeks later, with a personal loan approved, I owned a metallic brown Mitsubishi Scorpion Coupe. Oh, what a feeling! Oh, whoops – wrong brand!

This is as simple as goal-setting gets, harnessing the power of the RAS and arranging the mind. Neville said …

*'Health, wealth, beauty, and genius are not created; they are only manifested by the arrangement of the mind.'*

Clinical neuroscientist and psychiatrist Daniel G Amen, MD, founder of Amen Clinics and *New York Times* bestselling author, demonstrates how manifesting is grounded in and supported by science …

*'Focusing on your goals sparks brain activity, especially in the prefrontal cortex, the region of the brain involved in planning, forethought, and follow-through—the tools you need to realize your dreams. When you tell your prefrontal cortex what you want, it looks for ways to create that reality by helping you match your behaviour to your goals.'* Dr Amen's work goes on to say we should be looking for the 'micro moments of happiness' that happen throughout our day. By developing this habit, you train your brain to rewire itself to have a positivity bias. *'When you really pay attention to these micro moments, they can have a big impact on the neurochemicals of happiness—including dopamine, serotonin, and oxytocin—and enhance overall positivity.'* All of this reinforces that the subconscious can't tell fact from fantasy and will act on the instructions it receives – good or bad!

Let me also summarise the BOLVIS principle for you …

BOLVIS (The Eagle)

*Superhero Identity:* The Resilient Visionary

*Special Power:* To see the big picture from lofty heights

*Key Ability:* To recover from setbacks and persist

Create a BOLd VISion

WHY?

For the lack of a vision, people perish!

Develops assertiveness to remain emotionally resilient to challenges and setbacks.

Allows you to see the forest for the trees!

Switches on the reticular activating system (RAS) harnessing the power of the subconscious mind.

Creates abundance through eventual achievement.

WHAT?

Think big – be bold.

Get clarity on a 'compelling' future. Never give permission for anyone or anything to cause you to let go of what is right for you.

Grab and maximise opportunities.

SELF-LEADERSHIP & TEAM DYNAMICS APPLICATION:

*'ACHIEVING DESIRED OUTCOMES THROUGH CLARITY OF VISION AND PERSISTENCE.'*

© 2023 BOLVIS the eagle is copyright protected – Ian Stephens and enRich Training & Development Pty Ltd

# ABOUT IAN

IAN IS KNOWN AS the 'sales and mindset mastery guy'. He is the author of six books, including the award-winning *shiFt MINDSET – Why You're Not Getting What You Want and How to Create Desired Results … Faster!* Ian's twenty-plus years' experience of training and speaking in twenty-nine countries makes him an authority on topics like peak performance, sales and business development, change management, leadership and developing high-performing teams.

He is also an award-winning speaker and trainer having received the Educator of the Year Award and the prestigious Nevin Award from Professional Speakers Australia (PSA) in 2020. He was also inducted into the PSA Hall of Fame in 2022 in recognition of his contribution to the professional speaking industry in Australia.

# DR KATE MIRAN KIM
# UNLEASHING THE ENTREPRENEURIAL PASSION

*To achieve what you set out to do, you need will and motivation, challenge and perseverance, the strength to persevere with all your passion without giving up, and the courage to try again without succumbing to failure.*

## MY JOURNEY AS A VISIONARY LEADER

As I REFLECT ON my journey as an entrepreneur and advocate for women in the world of business, I am reminded of the powerful driving force that has fuelled my path – the passion for entrepreneurship. It's a passion that has guided me from the classroom to the boardroom, from motherhood to global initiatives. In this chapter, I'll share my personal story, my experiences and the transformative power of entrepreneurial passion.

My journey as a visionary leader began with a vision – an aspiration to empower women in entrepreneurship. I had the privilege of co-founding K-WEL (Korean Women Entrepreneurship Leaders) alongside seventy dedicated women CEOs who shared a common goal: creating an investment-friendly environment in our region. Daegu, our home base, became the nucleus of our efforts to foster a thriving local startup and investment ecosystem.

Our mission was clear – to support women who were determined to challenge the global market, overcoming not just local barriers but also the unique challenges faced by women in business. This was the genesis of my lifelong commitment to empower women in entrepreneurship.

## THE SEEDS OF SELF-MOTIVATION

The path into entrepreneurship was influenced by a profound observation I made in my late twenties. Running a language school specialising in strategy consulting for special-purpose high school entrance examinations, I had the privilege of working with many exceptional young minds. What struck me most was their self-motivation – the inner drive that propelled them to surmount countless obstacles on their path to success.

This observation ignited a spark within me. I became deeply passionate about designing educational content that could harness and nurture this innate motivation. My pursuit of this passion led me to further my studies, earning a master's degree in business administration. During this academic journey, the keyword that resonated with me was 'entrepreneurship'.

## FROM ACADEMIA TO ENTREPRENEURSHIP

My academic journey did not end with my MBA; it was just the beginning. I embarked on a challenging but rewarding path, pursuing a doctorate in educational technology. As a driven researcher and aspiring entrepreneur, I found myself at a crossroads during pregnancy and childbirth. It was a pivotal moment – one that would ultimately reshape my career.

Around one hundred days after giving birth, I founded Comma and Exclamation Mark Co Ltd, a company dedicated to corporate education and consulting. This venture was borne out of my experience as a highly educated professional who had to navigate a career break due to child care. It was during this challenging period that I found my true calling

– supporting women in their pursuit of entrepreneurship.

## UNLOCKING THE POTENTIAL OF WOMEN ENTREPRENEURS

The four years it took to complete my doctoral dissertation on women entrepreneurship were transformative. Balancing the demands of pregnancy, motherhood, starting a business and rigorous academic research, I pondered a fundamental question: Why did I want to return to work?

I realised that my desire to contribute to the professional world was not unique to me; there was a demand from countless other women looking to re-enter the workforce after career breaks or build their own businesses. I was determined to prove that women could thrive in entrepreneurship when provided with the right ecosystem and support.

My research journey led me to interview seven hundred successful women entrepreneurs, revealing distinct differences between women and men entrepreneurs. It became evident that we needed to explore innovative ways to blend business with the unique conditions of pregnancy, childbirth and child care. Creating an environment conducive to the success of women entrepreneurs became my mission – a turning point in the context of declining marriage rates and low birth rates.

## A LOCAL FOCUS WITH A GLOBAL OUTLOOK

While Daegu was the epicentre of our efforts, I recognised the need to think globally. Daegu-Gyeongbuk had a lower venture startup rate compared to other regions, largely due to a lack of support programs and professional manpower. The solution I envisioned was 'global'.

K-WEL embarked on a mission to attract international conventions and organisations to Daegu, creating global private investment opportunities. In 2019, WiSE24 brought together 25,000 participants, including accelerators, investors and forty-five teams from women-founded companies, hailing from fifteen countries. Our efforts were amplified through collaborations with organisations like the Daegu Center for Creative Economy and Innovation and 'Wslab', a women's entrepreneurship support organisation headquartered in Silicon Valley.

I designed initiatives such as the World League and Women's League at the Global Innovator Festa (GIF), further emphasising the importance of a global perspective in women's entrepreneurship.

## THE FAMILY THAT INSPIRES ME

As I navigate my roles as a woman entrepreneur, professor, mentor, accelerator, wife and mother, my family remains my greatest source of motivation. Being a mother has been both a strength and an inspiration. It's a role that has taught me to rise above challenges with resilience and determination. Witnessing the birth of other women entrepreneurs with my support has been profoundly fulfilling. It's a testament to the impact we can have on others when we extend a helping hand.

## THE PATH FORWARD: NURTURING ENTREPRENEURIAL SPIRIT

The recent declaration of 2023 as the 'era of austerity' by economists presents a formidable challenge. Economic hardships compounded by the long COVID-19 pandemic may cast a shadow of poverty over many lives. In such trying times, the importance of entrepreneurial education – a powerful tool for overcoming economic challenges – has never been more significant.

I firmly believe that we can create entrepreneurs who will not yield to difficult economic conditions, but rather forge their own path with courage. This conviction fuels my commitment to building a robust Korean startup ecosystem. K-WEL, comprising individuals with diverse motives and successful startup experiences, stands ready to share our knowledge, encourage new challenges and empower more women to realise their dreams.

## EMBRACING THE SPIRIT OF CHUTZPAH

In my journey, I've had the privilege of learning from President Hezki Arieli, my mentor from Global Excellence in Israel. He affectionately calls me 'Jinji', a reference to my red hair. Israel's *chutzpah* – a spirit of boldness, shamelessness and resilience – resonated with me. This national identity, rooted in learning from failure, constant inquiry and a global market mindset, has been an invaluable source of inspiration.

Through in-depth conversations with President Arieli, an authority on creative education, I've translated my learnings from the home of chutzpah into entrepreneurship. I've come to understand that entrepreneurship is a force that empowers individuals to willingly challenge their plans, armed with motivation, determination and the courage to persist.

## CONCLUSION: THE POWER OF ENTREPRENEURIAL PASSION

In an era marked by uncertainty and economic challenges, the entrepreneurial spirit shines as a beacon of hope. It is a power that propels individuals to confront adversity head-on, to persevere with unwavering passion and to embrace failure as a stepping stone to success. This spirit isn't confined to entrepreneurs alone; it's a vital force for all individuals navigating the complexities of our times.

As we embrace the era of austerity, the importance of entrepreneurship education becomes increasingly evident. It is through education that we instil the courage to start without hesitation, the resilience to face adversity and the strength to forge a path forward. My mission, my passion and the legacy of K-WEL are all aligned with this vision.

## TAKEAWAY 1: ENTREPRENEURIAL SPIRIT AS A BEACON OF HOPE

In my own journey, I've witnessed how the entrepreneurial spirit becomes a guiding light in times of uncertainty and economic challenges. It's a force that propels individuals to confront adversity head-on, much like the way it did for me. This spirit is a reminder that, no matter the obstacles we encounter, having a deep passion for entrepreneurship can ignite the determination needed to persevere, and ultimately, transform adversity into opportunities.

## TAKEAWAY 2: ENTREPRENEURSHIP EDUCATION FOR EMPOWERMENT

I firmly believe in the transformative power of entrepreneurship education. It's through education that we can instil the courage to take that initial step, the resilience to weather setbacks and the strength to forge a unique path forward. In today's world, marked by economic uncertainties and challenges, this type of education is essential in empowering individuals to navigate complex situations, even during times of austerity. My commitment to this vision underscores the profound impact education can have in enabling individuals to embrace entrepreneurship as a means of personal and economic growth.

## TAKEAWAY 3: THE UNIVERSAL RELEVANCE OF ENTREPRENEURIAL PASSION

While my journey is rooted in the context of women's entrepreneurship in South Korea, the message I want to convey transcends borders. Entrepreneurial passion isn't confined to business owners alone; it's a force that can drive success and resilience in any field or endeavour. As readers, I encourage you to draw inspiration from my experiences and recognise that the entrepreneurial spirit is a valuable asset for navigating the challenges of our ever-evolving world. It equips us to face uncertainty with determination and optimism, regardless of our specific circumstances or locations.

# ABOUT DR KATE

Director Kate Miran Kim of K-WEL works as Korea's first global women entrepreneurship expert.

In addition, she shares her experiences by publishing books such as *There Is an Answer to Future Talent Entrepreneurship* and *The Magic of The Library*. Established by seventy women CEOs who share the same will for creating an investment environment in the region, K-WEL is based in Daegu and takes the lead in creating a healthy local startup and investment ecosystem, making entrepreneurship start concentrating on other regions beside the capital.

Director Kim has been supporting women who challenge the global market by overcoming the two obstacles of local and women.

'Since my late twenties, I have been running a language school specializing in strategy consulting for special-purpose high school entrance examination, and I have been able to meet many children who have achieved achievements in their teens. One common feature I found while meeting children was self-motivation. The clear motivation the children found on their own was becoming the driving force behind them overcoming numerous obstacles in the process of reaching their goals.'

Having a dream of designing educational contents related to motivation herself, director Kim deepened her studies by obtaining a doctorate in educational technology following her master's degree in business administration. The keyword she found in the process was 'entrepreneurship'.

Director Kim, who continued her research while immersed in entrepreneurship, not only took a doctorate course during pregnancy and childbirth, but also founded, around one hundred days after giving birth, Comma and Exclamation Mark Co, Ltd, a company specialising in corporate education and consulting. And the experience at the time, which was not easy, became an opportunity for director Kim to turn her eyes to a new field. Even though she was a highly educated person with a master's and doctoral degree and a professional career of more than ten years, she experienced a period of career break due to childcare, and witnessed cases of difficulties in re-employment or entrepreneurship.

The four years that it took for director Kim Mi-Ran to publish her doctoral dissertation on women entrepreneurship gave her a new direction. While being pregnant, raising children, starting a business and studying at the same time, she focused on the question, 'Why do I want to work again?'

Director Kim, who recalled the sense of achievement in her prime, came to the idea that there must be a demand from other woman to overcome the period of career break or to build her own career besides herself. And she began to focus on what factors have helped so many career women overcome difficult times and achieve new achievements. Director Kim explained that she wanted to prove that women can succeed as long as the ecosystem and conditions for starting a business are met. 'I interviewed seven hundred successful women entrepreneurs while writing my doctoral dissertation. I was able to check the women entrepreneurship naturally. Women entrepreneurs are clearly different from men entrepreneurs. There is a need to think about ways to combine business with the special conditions of pregnancy, childbirth and child care. I thought that creating an environment that could produce successful women entrepreneurs could present a turning point for the recent trend of nonmarriage and low birth rates. To do so, women entrepreneurs need training to find and maximize the strengths that only women have, such as Market Kurly, Grip and JiguInCompany.'

Director Kim focused on the uniqueness of Daegu, which is a region that has a unique conservative tendency. Daegu-Gyeongbuk's venture startup rate is remarkably low compared to other cities and provinces.

She diagnosed that the number of people leaving the region is increasing due to support programs that are not connected to start-up related activities centered on the metropolitan area and the lack of professional manpower.

In this situation, the breakthrough she found was 'global'. K-WEL is creating global private investment opportunities by attracting international conventions and organisations such as WiSE24, APEC, GIF, and G100 to Daegu. In 2019, 25,000 participants, including accelerators and investors from all over the world, as well as forty-five teams from companies founded or run by women, coming from fifteen countries including the United States, Brazil and Taiwan, participated both online and offline to share their experiences in 'WiSE24' co-hosted by Comma and Exclamation Mark Co, Ltd.

At the Daegu Center for Creative Economy and Innovation and 'Wslab,' a women's entrepreneurship support organization headquartered in Silicon Valley, USA. Director Kim said that it was an opportunity for many women entrepreneurs to meet more than 100 global investors. Having designed the World League and Women's League at the Global Innovator Festa (GIF) at EXCO in Daegu last year, she plans to continue her activities as the Business Accelerator Korea Chair of The Club G100, a non-profit organization where CEOs of world-class companies gather and conduct business networking.

Director Kim Mi-Ran, who is busy working as a woman entrepreneur, professor, mentor, accelerator, wife and mother, says that the biggest driving force is her family. Among them, being a 'mother' was the strength that brought her difficulties at times and at the same time allowed her to constantly stand up again without getting frustrated in the face of many

difficulties. In addition, watching the birth of another woman entrepreneur with her own little help allowed her to feel a sense of accomplishment. In fact, it is a picture of creating a spin-off company by encouraging employees belonging to Comma and Exclamation Mark Co, Ltd. to start a business. 'It is a great pleasure and reward for me to be active in this region and contribute to creating a startup ecosystem. Seeing local entrepreneurs winning awards is overwhelming in itself, but I am grateful and rewarded because it can become another driving force and give birth to numerous women entrepreneurs.'

Recently, the Ministry of SMEs and Startups announced that the venture fund recorded the highest performance by surpassing ten trillion won for the first time. Support for the growth of women-owned businesses and strengthening their competitiveness is also on the rise. Director Kim welcomed the situation where investment in venture companies is spreading from to other regions and women, but she made it clear that the

Ministry of SMEs and Startups needs to be prepared to face these changes. It explains that the women entrepreneurship ecosystem can be more active when founders take an interest in them and think about it in solidarity with an active attitude.

Hezki Arieli, president of Global Excellence in Israel, who is Kim's mentor, says he calls her 'Jinji' (red hair). 'I have heard a lot about Israel's "chutzpah" story, a powerhouse of talent development and startups. It seems to be the same concept as "spirit" in Korea, but it actually means shameless or bold. The national identity of learning from failure, constantly asking questions, and using the world stage as a market from the start is a point worthy of emulation.'

Director Kim added that she was able to build the foundation for talented and successful people equipped with boldness, regardless of victory and defeat, and that she was able to sublimate the many learnings and realisations she gained from a philosopher in Israel, the home of chutzpah, into entrepreneurship through an in-depth talk with President Hezki Arieli, an authority on creative education.

'Entrepreneurship can be said to be the power that can make someone to challenge what he/she has planned, willingly. To achieve what you set out to do, you need will and motivation, challenge and perseverance, the strength to persevere with all your passion without giving up, and the courage to try again without succumbing to failure. The process of constantly finding this kind of mind within oneself is a necessary spirit not only for entrepreneurs but also for all people living in this era.'

An economist recently named 2023 the 'era of austerity.' It is a prospect that the economic blow added to the long COVID-19 pandemic may cause an era of austerity in which people will have to endure this situation beyond poverty. Director Kim Mi-Ran emphasised that the importance of education on entrepreneurship, which is the power to overcome the era of austerity, is on the rise.

It was with the conviction that it would be possible to create entrepreneurs who would not give in to difficult economic conditions and forge their own path we give them courage to start without hesitation and instill the power into them to move toward the future by the creation of a proper Korean startup ecosystem. K-WEL, a group of players with their own motives and experiences of successful startups, is willing to share their experiences and encourage new challenges. I expect more women to realize their own dreams and stand tall in the center of the world economy with K-WEL.

# HARTINI BINTI OSMAN
# A BRIEF WRITE-UP ABOUT DHO

*To be successful, just know yourself, trust your instincts, be brave, be visible and dream big!*

MY NAME IS HARTINI Binti Osman, a president and group managing director of a company known as Prihatin Ehsan Holdings Sdn Bhd. I am also a G100 global chair – philanthropy, business and poverty eradication in Malaysia and a president, ASEAN – India Business Council, WICCI.

I was born in Alor Setar, Kedah, on 2 June 1968 and grew up with supportive family who encouraged me to pursue business at an early age. I started early in life, got married in my teenage years, yet still prospered in my work and could manage my study well until being accepted into Harvard Business School (HBS) advance management program AMP 190 where I managed to learn many things in a short time of study. At HBS I blossomed in nearly all my undertakings. I was awarded with many successful achievements while going through many facets of my life. I got married to a caring and supportive husband and was blessed with nine wonderful children. Now I am a happy granny with eleven beautiful and handsome grandchildren.

What more do we want in life? Happiness, great health and the ability to help people as many as we can, spreading peace and love.

I started my own business at the age of twenty-three, and after facing a lot of obstacles, adversities and challenges, I become what I am today – a successful businesswoman, leader and philanthropist.

## BEING A BUSINESSWOMAN, LEADER AND PHILANTHROPIST

We know that success doesn't happen overnight but is, and always will be, the culmination of a lot of hard work. What inspired me in life is determination, perseverance, doing what is right and trying to focus on what we are good at and love doing. Sometimes we feel that we can do everything, but we won't be able to do everything ourselves. We will need a team of people, support and love. We will also need to learn how and what makes us good to ensure that whatever we do will be successful. But along the way we will always face obstacles such as the people around us, the funds, the authorities, the client and the support team, our staff/team, our supplier and contractors. Administrating means that we need to ensure that we have a checklist and guidelines on how we want to mitigate the occurred issues or problems.

In doing something we wouldn't know all the methods, the rules, the requirements. We will have an instinct that we want to do the right thing in our way. We listen to others and will go through the process; we will be able to do that but often we will have to go through a very lengthy process in making things that are supposed to be much easier for us to achieve but we will be doing it in a longer way as we won't be able to know because we are not guided. As for example, being an entrepreneur, we must be able to know, what we want to do, for example in selling products. We need to focus on learning about the product and how to tackle buyers. We love what we are doing because once we love our doing then we are able to convince buyers to buy our products. Being an entrepreneur is not only about selling a product, a program or anything that people desired to own, I think we must learn to ensure that we will be able to get the customer and volume that we want, our target.

## LOOKING FORWARD

Nobody can say for sure if they were born to be a leader. Leaders have always been viewed as fundamentally different from other people. There are many people who are smart, ambitious and extroverted. We had to encourage ourselves to think independently and provide a values system that encouraged hard work, ethics, consideration for others and determination. We know that a legendary leader continues to look forward, unfazed by any barriers, obstacles or missteps along the way. We continue to pursue good strategies and to focus on the future rather than be distracted by present challenges and obstacles. Leadership requires action and the passion to put the effort into turning the good idea into a sustainable revenue machine.

## CONFIDENCE AND ASSERTIVENESS

I can say that building confidence and assertiveness is essential for all in leadership, especially women. How to build this? Firstly, by setting clear goals and breaking them into manageable steps, you can boost confidence as each milestone is achieved. Secondly, practising effective communication and public speaking helps in articulating ideas assertively. By seeking out opportunities to lead projects and embracing challenges, any person, especially women, can gradually enhance their self-assurance and authoritative presence, solidifying their effectiveness as leaders.

I can also see that people, especially women, in leadership often possess qualities that make them adept at nurturing the next generation. Empathy and active listening create an inclusive and supportive environment. Effective communication and collaboration help them convey knowledge and encourage teamwork. Their resilience and ability to multitask set an example for balancing responsibilities. By embodying these attributes, leaders inspire and guide emerging talents, fostering an environment of growth and empowerment.

## NETWORKING AND INSPIRATION

Networking and mentorship are crucial for people's, especially women's, growth in leadership. Networking expands their circle, exposing them to new ideas and opportunities. Engaging with peers and mentors provides insights into different leadership styles, fostering personal growth. Mentorship offers guidance from experienced leaders, accelerating skill development and helping them navigate challenges. Both networking and mentorship empower people, especially women, to broaden their influence, gain valuable perspectives and achieve their leadership aspirations. I'm also inspired by seeing companies or organisations, communities and people succeed.

## CONSTANTLY EVOLVING

For me, a leader should be dynamic and not static. We should continue evolving to stay relevant. We should not be simply satisfied with the success we have achieved to date but to heed the lessons of failure. Therefore, continuous learning and skill development are pivotal in propelling people, especially women, to success in leadership. As industries evolve, learning new skills keeps them competitive and adaptable. Acquiring fresh knowledge broadens their perspective, enabling them to innovate and make strategic decisions. This commitment to learning inspires confidence and earns the respect of peers and subordinates, ultimately shaping all leaders, especially women, into well- rounded and influential figures.

## HELPING OTHERS BY GIVING BACK

An admirable leader has taken charge to help others by guiding them in the right direction, imparting knowledge and experience, or even providing the necessary resources that will improve the lives or careers of others. I have always taken a selfless approach to my leadership, spending considerable money and time in philanthropic efforts to give to others.

An example of philanthropy is G100 Club. G100 is an eminent and empowered club of one hundred powerful women leaders in the world across one hundred diverse sectors, with a vision for the future. G100 comprises a league of luminaries of eminence and excellence including Nobel laureates, heads of states, ministers, businesswomen, philanthropists, investors, entrepreneurs, corporate and community leaders. Each G100 wing is led by a global chair.

I am a G100 global chair for philanthropy, business and poverty eradication, Malaysia. Our vision is to create and build a caring global community to eradicate persistent poverty by encouraging HNIs, businesses, foundations and organisations to give back to society for supporting vital needs of food, shelter, health, security, education, empowerment and capacity building of people in underserved sections of society, especially girls and women.

Philanthropy means generosity in all its forms and is often defined as giving gifts of time, talent and treasure to help make life better for other people. In other words, a philanthropist is someone who donates their time, money and reputation to charitable causes and cares for someone else's needs before their own. For example, giving food to a person who is suffering from a famine is charity. The food helps the person for a short period of time, but the person will become hungry again in the future. Teaching the person how to grow food is philanthropy because it eliminates the social problem causing the person's hunger. It is more long-term and strategic which focuses on helping people and solving their problem over the long-term. We know that ending poverty is not just helping the unfortunate or less-able people. It is giving every person, especially women, the chance to live with dignity. So, we are building forward together, ending persistent poverty and respecting all people.

Overall I can say that 'overcoming poverty is not a gesture of charity'. It is the protection of a fundamental human right, the right to dignity and a decent life. Protection of a fundamental human right, the right to dignity and a decent life with quote 'while poverty persists, there is no true freedom'.

In line with our vision, we encourage people, especially women, to take up education, skills training and guidance to enable them to get jobs, upgrade their socioeconomy and achieve wellbeing/prosperous life. For example, one of my and my team's efforts in education is our Mobile School Program. This program is very comprehensive and beneficial, and it has been implemented in Petaling Jaya, Selangor, Malaysia, with positive feedback from participants and parents became a spirit for the facilitators to further refine the module and plan to bring this program to higher scale for the benefit of young children, especially school students, in building their spirit and personality. Focus is given to aspects of positive self-development, career building and the setting of participants' life goals.

As we all know, to bring growth and prosperity in a society, the path that wiser people take, is of peace and harmony. Without peace and harmony in a nation, it is impossible to achieve political strength, economic stability or cultural growth. Countries with greater gender equality are more connected, helps prevent violence and makes our communities safer, healthier and have better wellbeing.

In return, as a leader and a philanthropist, I receive happiness and satisfaction by knowing that I am providing benefits that can create the leaders of the future who will then shape the world for those generations to come. It was about driving significant change in the world that would make a difference for those who need it the most. I agree with Bill Gates, who quoted, 'As we look ahead into the next century, leaders will be those who empower others.'

## JOURNEY TO FUTURE PROSPERITY

Prosperity is defined as the state of success, wealth and good fortune. So how we could achieve prosperity?

We know that challenges and obstacles are part of leadership, growth and success. I believed that success is the outcome of hard and consistent work, strong determination, yielding results and over time.

My greatest challenges have been the moments where I am navigating personal circumstances while also being in high demand at work. The confluence of personal and work responsibilities can be very challenging to figure out how to balance those demands. And I understand that it is tricky to maintain a work-life balance. So, we have to plan and organise our time properly.

We have to be a leader with integrity and need to create the conditions for success happen to us. We all know that integrity and innovation are both built on the foundation of trust. For example, our staff will not tell us the truth if they are afraid of our response. So that can lead to a lack of integrity and opportunity for our business.

In order to keep our staff motivated, we need to know them, spend time with them and know what motivates them but not what we want them to be motivated by. We must build joy into the work and create ways for the staff to shine.

In my journey to future prosperity, I have always been clear that I wanted to be a difference-maker in organisations that are committed to making a difference in the community. Therefore, I must always push myself to diversify my ideas and approaches and to be bold about the solutions that I offer.

My personal goal is to continue to lead forward, find new boundaries and bust through ceilings that haven't been broken. I'm going to consistently seek opportunities for growth and ways to lend my leadership skills.

You also can be a successful person, just know yourself, trust your instincts, be brave, be visible and dream big!

# ABOUT HARTINI

DATIN DR (H.C.) HAJAH Hartini Binti Osman is the president and group managing director of Prihatin Group of Companies, Malaysia. She is also the G100 global chair – philanthropy, business and poverty eradication in Malaysia and a president, ASEAN – India Business Council, WICCI.

She was born in Alor Setar, Kedah on 2 June 1968 and grew up with supportive family who encouraged her in doing business at an early age. She started early in life, got married in her teen years yet still she prospers in her work and could well manage her study until being accepted in Harvard Business School (HBS) and in Advance Management Programme AMP 190 where she managed to learn many things in such a short time of study in HBS and blossomed in nearly all her undertakings. She was awarded with many successful achievements while going through many facets of her life. She got married to a caring and supportive husband and was blessed with nine wonderful children and with eleven great grandchildren.

Datin Dr. holds a number of positions in Prihatin's subsidiary group company and affiliated business that specialise in the hotelier and investment industries, as developers and contractors, facility management, project management, property management, foundations, NGOs and cooperatives.

She is the exco member and Alumni of Harvard Business School Alumni Club Malaysia and Alumni for (AMP 190) Advance Management Programme Harvard Business School. She is also the Associate Member of Gayong Heirs Meor Rahman for Malaysian Gayong Martial Arts Organization (Pertubuhan Seni Silat Gayong Malaysia).

She has received various awards and recognitions, among them are the Winner for Trading Sector by NAWEM during The NAWEM Women Entrepreneur Award, Sandang Mahkota Seri Cahaya Pelangi, Sandang Kehormat Kebesaran Silat Seni Gayong Malaysia No. 55 from Pertubuhan Seni Silat Gayong Malaysia, Doctor of Philosophy in martial arts science by the World Academy of Martial Arts Philosophy and Science (WAMAPS), Women of the Decade by Women Economic Forum (WEF) and Doctor of Philosophy (Honoris Causa) from RAI University India.

She achieved success and achievement as the Malaysia Country Chair for Corporate Governance G100, G100 Global Chair, Philanthropy, Business & Poverty Eradication, President, ASEAN – India Business Council under the Women's Indian Chamber of Commerce And Industry (WICCI), Vice Head of UMNO Women of Hulu Selangor and Honorary Advisor (I) for Persatuan Usahawan Wawasan Wanita Malaysia (Wawasanita).

Her future program that is currently being planned is Collaboration In The Development of Robotic and Automation Programs and Others between Yayasan Bina Kesejahteraan (YBCare), Yayasan Basmi Kemiskinan (YBK), Chatbots.expert South Africa and Selangor Human Resources Development Centre (SHRDC).

In addition to being involved in business, she also involved in poverty eradication programs under YBK, wel-being and volunteering works under YBCare. She also lead a cooperative in doing business and agro which part of the profit channelled for CSR program.

She aspires to launch a philanthropic funds to able her to support many programme with all G100 country chair in her wings for current and future sustainable programme to assist in eradication of poverty.

# AILSA PAGE
# THE ACCIDENTAL BUSINESS LEADER

*Don't be afraid to do things your way.*

## INTRODUCTION AND BACKGROUND

I'M AILSA PAGE, AND I'm an accidental business owner but it's been one long accident given I've run my own and other businesses for over twenty-five years. I'm also a small business advocate, trainer and consultant and a qualified professional marketer with qualifications in psychology, management and training. I'm also an author, speaker, musician and occasional tap dancer.

I am one of two girls in my family, and we moved around a lot as children following my Dad's work. I'd lived in six different places by the time I was seven. We didn't move after that, but learning how to build connections with different people and communities has been a big theme in my life.

I've always been a go-getter and was a natural marketer as a young person, although the word marketing didn't really exist in my world at that time. I had many jobs when I was growing up and throughout university. When I finished my studies, I worked in the government and not-for-profit sectors in various roles. It was only later, when I was studying marketing and marketing strategy at the Melbourne Business School that it became clear that all the roles I'd held to date were actually marketing roles – they just weren't called that in non-business sectors! So, I guess you could say I officially became a marketer shortly after and was recognised by the Australian Marketing Institute in 1996.

I stumbled upon the world of business during my first marriage. My husband at the time was an entrepreneur and owned several businesses. I learnt a lot about how business works, the highs and the lows, and I adored working and developing marketing in his business. I had found my happy place trying new marketing tactics and seeing them work. At the same time, I started working with programs and organisations that helped businesses such as business enterprise programs, business associations and innovation centres, I was also running my own training business part-time. I was hooked and further dived into the world of business ownership when I started full-time in my own marketing consulting business in 1999 which is still going strong today. Since then, I've owned a couple of other businesses including a wine shop and developed several business ventures with business partners. I've definitely found a tribe of people I love – business owners.

Right from the start, my appetite for all things small business was insatiable. I wanted to know more. I read voraciously, attended any seminar that was going – there weren't a lot back then, this was BZ (before Zoom) – and joined business networks and associations. Luckily, I learnt a lot through the jobs I had. I then later ran my own business workshops, taught at universities, designed business training programs for government, helped other businesses, consulted to government and judged business awards. So I got to where I am as a leader in small business because I was passionate, observant, knowledgeable, experienced, opinionated and vocal. People liked to hear what I had to say.

## VISION AND INSPIRATION

My vision is for all voices to be represented, particularly those that are not often heard and less powerful but no less important. That we can listen and learn from all experiences and expertise, not just the loudest.

That our uniqueness and individuality is celebrated and we are not forced to conform to 'the one way' (usually the traditional, or often male, way) of doing things.

I didn't become a leader by design, it just happened. I just wanted to ensure that I provided a different opinion and perspective in business. When I was first starting in business, consulting was a very male-dominated industry. Most of the business consultants were men of a certain age. They had similar backgrounds and approaches to business and shared a view about what business success looked like. My approach, beliefs and idea of success were different. My reasons for starting my own business were a reaction to the constrictions of the workforce at the time. I didn't like that workplaces tended to favour men. Women were often spoken over and not given credit for their ideas, promoted less and often paid less. My desire to run my own business was to ensure that I had freedom to create and be credited for my ideas, rewarded for my work efforts, and to have flexibility to incorporate the important priorities in my life with my work. This seems so normal now but a quarter of a century ago there were not that many businesses based from home.

I wanted to be the alternative voice for business owners. The one that says you can do business your way. Work out what's important to you and build your business around that, rather than comparing yourself to a standard you may not even value. I wanted to engender hope, create joy and fun in business and encourage people to embrace their differences and uniqueness rather than trying to blend in and fit into a model that doesn't serve them (or their business). I had seen doing it differently work for both business owners and their businesses. I therefore wanted to encourage people to choose difference rather than conformity. More recently I've extended this message specifically to marketing. There is so much bad marketing out there because everyone is doing the same thing indiscriminately and burning up their time, money and energy without getting results.

I relish people being self-reliant with opportunities for self-determination. To me, business can provide this. It is just important to maintain your values and not blindly subscribe to traditional business goals of money, power and status.

## PASSION AND DRIVE

I'm passionate about the individual experience being validated. I get highly frustrated when every business or businessowner is labelled as one in the same. For me even making the assumption that all women in business have the same experience or struggle with the same things gets me riled. Like all individuals there are many different and unique experiences. It's good to find similarities but also to acknowledge differences. In business it's often the big voices that are heard and they do not necessarily reflect many of the other business owners. I think providing another point of view is something that I do a lot in my life. I guess I don't tolerate broad generalisations. There are always exceptions to the rule.

Can you recall a specific moment or experience that ignited your passion for leadership?

I've always been encouraged to stand up and speak out and never to be afraid of leadership. Both my parents were leaders in their communities, and they encourage me to do the same. I received the message very early on that someone has to be the leader – why not you? It was seen as normal, and I got the confidence from a very young age to put my hand up. To be captain, to be student representative, to be president to be school captain.

I have many memories of my mother at the end of a ballet concert or event standing up and saying, 'On behalf of everyone I'd just like to thank/say/do …' As children, my sister and I would often cringe at this but in hindsight, what a great role model she was for us. I, like my mother, have always felt it is important to speak up for the underdog – for the quiet voices that don't always have the opportunity to be heard.

My passion is to amplify the voices that are often drowned out, that other point of view of those that swim against the tide.

## KEY ACCOMPLISHMENTS

- Universal Business School of Sydney Fellowship Award in recognition of a distinguished contribution to entrepreneurship in Australia.
- Telstra Business Awards and Telstra Women's Business Awards judge for seven years.
- Specialist judge for the Australian Marketing Institute's 'National Marketing Excellence' awards.
- Australian Business Arts Foundation Awards for Business and Arts Partnership awarded by the Prime Minister of Australia.
- President Professional Speakers Australia Victorian Chapter President.
- Winner Business & Professional Services Star Women in Business Awards.
- Highest accreditation and international designation of Certified Speaking Professional with Professional Speakers Australia.

## SIGNIFICANT ACHIEVEMENTS AS A LEADER

- Working with programs for rural women in business, asylum seekers and new migrants, developing and delivering workshops for state government.
- During COVID working with councils to help inform, support and encourage business owners through a series of webinars and timely videos.
- Regular contributor to business magazines/blogs in Australia.

## HOW DID MY PASSION CONTRIBUTE TO THESE ACCOMPLISHMENTS?

I love what I do and when you do something for a long time you look back and realise that there has been a lot of achievements. Curiosity gets you moving and if you love what you do you can do it for a long time.

## OVERCOMING CHALLENGES

When you have something to say that goes against popular thinking. This is challenging as you start to question yourself. You don't get booked because your message isn't popular or when you are not in fashion – e.g. woman when people want men, older when people are looking for young, etc. It is hard not to take it personally.

When you come up against ignorance for example when dealing with bureaucrats or people who have a limited experience of what it's like to be in business. They make assumptions, decisions or policies that make life difficult. I know it's through limited or lack of exposure and experience but it's still really frustrating having to wait until they gain that insight for themselves.

Burnout – going against the stream can take more energy. Sometimes you feel as though you are beating your head against a brick wall. It's important to be mindful of your energy levels and find ways to rest and rejuvenate.

Feeling alone. Sometimes an overwhelming sense of loneliness when you think you are the only person who feels this passionate about these issues. I'm reminded of the fairytale *The Emperor's Got New Clothes* where the little boy goes against the crowd to speak his truth and is frustrated that no one else seems to see what he is seeing. In the fairy tale the towns-folk were frightened of standing up to the King and speaking the truth. If they had been a different group of people the fairy tale may never have been written. So for me if you are starting to feel as though you are the only one who thinks a certain way – it's time to find some different people to hang out with.

Neglecting other parts of your life – you can easily get carried away with your passion to the detriment of other parts of your life. In small doses this is not such a problem but if it's for longer periods of time it can pull life out of balance like your health, family, friends and other priorities in your life.

## HOW DID I OVERCOME THESE CHALLENGES, AND WHAT DID I LEARN FROM THEM?

Learnt that I always have to keep stimulated and continually learning.

Wait for the tide to turn, and it will – be ready for opportunities when they do come your way rather than trying to plan and create things to turn out the way you want.

Team up with others – it is so much easier when there is a team than when it's just you.

Follow the joy. Connect with the parts of life, work, your mission that you enjoy and lean in to that. Avoid negative people, negative situations and take a break and focus on self-care if you are burnt-out. Create a routine of self-care rather than wait till burnout to do crisis care rather than maintenance.

## LEADERSHIP STYLE AND VALUES

- Connection – important to create connections with people, being able to communicate simply and find a common language.
- Respect – respecting differences and working with people that respect me.
- Truth – always tell the truth, always seek the truth even if it's difficult.
- Continual improvement – seek feedback, ongoing learning, review.
- Fun – collaborations, being creative, using humour, laughing at what it is to be human.

## TEAM BUILDING AND COLLABORATION

I respect people's different talents and experience and let them lead in their area. This can be a both a strength and weakness. I believe people when they say they can do something and let them just get on with the job. I'm not a micromanager so prefer to get a gun team of people with their specialist skills and then meet to look at particular problems to be solved from multiple perspectives.

If you are not having fun it just doesn't get done. So for me I try to make being in a team an enjoyable experience blending social and work.

## INNOVATION AND ADAPTABILITY

I love to gain feedback from customers and stakeholders. Research can help you improve and often sparks new ideas and innovation. Research can be formal or just listening.

I have come from a live performance background, and the ability to be flexible, think on your feet and adapt to a situation was the difference between success and failure in performance. Focusing on the outcome you want to achieve rather than being attached to the process or method of achieving it can be really important. Once, we arrived without my instrument which is a core part of the performance – there was no time to go back and retrieve it, the audience was waiting, they expected a show and we just had to give them that (with just one instrument). The important thing here was to entertain, so that's what we focused on – we entertained in a slightly different way to normal (yes, I pulled out a lot of tap dancing that day rather than play the piano) but the audience was none the wiser and enjoyed the show! We once played for a funeral and were given the brief of playing some serious classical music at the beginning. On the day, the organiser came and said the classical music was too sad – so we pivoted and played our more upbeat music slightly slower for the first set and then at a faster pace for the second set. No classical music got played that day!

## MENTORSHIP AND INFLUENCE

I've had three very influential mentors in my business journey. One was my first business coach who opened the door on a lot of opportunities including judging Australia's prestigious business awards. Then later, two older women in business I used to meet regularly who provided such great wisdom, humour and encouragement. I always remember the wise words of one of my mentors Brenda when I was questioning how long before I reach success in business – she said ten years. I was shocked at the time (as I was about seven years in) but she was right, and I often say that to many of the businesses I work with.

As a marketing and small business lecturer and trainer I have taught many business owners. I have certainly seen many of those businesses go onto greater heights. One of my proudest and most memorable moments was when I was giving a talk in regional Australia and one of the business owners in the audience came up and introduced himself. He was a former student, saw that I was speaking and wanted to come and tell me that it was my classes that inspired him to start his own business!

## LEGACY AND IMPACT

I just want to see more balanced happy, thriving small businesses and business owners.

People to be more willing to accept difference and to find ways to connect with each other.

A more balanced life for Australians.

## HOW DO YOU MEASURE THE IMPACT OF YOUR LEADERSHIP ON YOUR FIELD OR INDUSTRY?

- Longevity of ideas – will my ideas still hold up in twenty years?
- People circling back to your original ideas.
- Continued relevance and resonance with your peers and contemporaries.
- People still reading your book and finding it helpful.

## ADVICE FOR ASPIRING LEADERS

- Be the best you can be in your area.
- Take up leadership roles when they present themselves.
- Take it a day at a time.
- Have confidence in yourself and surround yourself with people that will support you.

## ARE THERE ANY KEY PRINCIPLES OR PRACTICES THAT HAVE BEEN INSTRUMENTAL IN YOUR SUCCESS?

- Having a coach.
- Regular reviews of my direction.
- Coming back to self – aligning actions with my values, allocating time to my priorities taking time out to reflect.
- Be yourself and do it your way.

## CLOSING THOUGHTS

I feel as though my leadership journey was not a conscious one. I pursued what I was passionate about and taking up opportunities as they arose and felt within my capacity. I don't feel as though the journey is over and it may well take a new direction. I'm on a long break at the moment the longest holiday I've had in thirty years! It's a self-care, relaxing, unwinding break from twenty-five years of go, go, go. It feels like the end of a chapter in a book and I'm not sure if there will be a new book, a sequel or just another chapter to be written when my holiday ends. Whatever happens I will be following my passion.

# ABOUT AILSA

I AM A PROFESSIONAL marketer, marketing consultant, workshop presenter, keynote speaker and author of three small business marketing books.

Passionate supporter of small business for twenty-plus years specialising in finding your point of difference with easy to understand strategies and techniques that get results.

I've helped hundreds of small- to medium-sized businesses and organisations dramatically improve their bottom line either by sales, membership base, or profile. Importantly, I know what it takes to succeed in small business (after all, AP Marketing Works has been going strong since 1999). I know what works, and what doesn't.

I have a business head and a gypsy heart, which is why even though Melbourne is my home base, I have a sweet spot for helping businesses interstate and in Victorian regional areas such as Mildura, Shepparton, Hamilton, Gippsland, Bendigo and Geelong.

When you work with me, we work together. You have access to my trusted marketing suppliers and contacts. I make it my business to get to know your business – and your customers – inside and out, so I can devise a strategy that gets real measurable results.

# AMANDA THOMPSON
# EMBRACING THE
# UNCONVENTIONAL

*Being financially fit is not just about crunching numbers and chasing*
*dollars. It is a journey; one of discovery, perseverance and self-discipline.*

WE LIVE IN A world of leadership, where stability and conformity often take precedence. However, I believe, the reality of leadership is far from linear. It's a profound journey where the unexpected becomes the norm, and the trials and triumphs of our personal lives serve as the most potent teachers.

This chapter delves into my world as a leader who dares to challenge the norm, not confined by the traditional definitions of authority but propelled by a passion to transform and empower. It's a world where leadership transcends titles and evolves into stories where resilience, empathy and adaptability take centrestage and is then the catalyst for transformation and empowerment.

Life has a funny way of teaching us the most valuable lessons when we least expect it, catching us off guard and reshaping the very core of who we are. My journey as a leader has been profoundly influenced by the trials and triumphs I've experienced in my personal life. These lessons have not only shaped my leadership style but also redefined my approach to financial planning.

From the outside, my path may seem like a carefully orchestrated progression in the financial industry. However, beneath the surface, my journey was marked by unforeseen challenges that served as invaluable teachers. Each obstacle, each unexpected twist and every moment of adversity became a pivotal chapter in my leadership story. I am an individual who has not only mastered the art of leadership but have also infused my unique life experiences into my leadership style.

This journey through the trials and triumphs of life has shaped me into the unconventional leader I am today. It's a role I embrace with passion and commitment, knowing that leadership is not just about authority but about making a meaningful impact on the lives of those I serve. Here are some key pieces of advice I've garnered from my experiences:

## THE CATALYST OF RESILIENCE IN THE FACE OF ADVERSITY

One of the most impactful lessons life bestowed upon me was the significance of resilience. The trials I faced were not just ripples in the pond; they were storms that threatened to capsize my boat. Leadership, I realised, is not merely steering during calm seas but braving the fiercest of storms with resilience as your guiding star. These experiences have taught me that resilience is a prerequisite for success. My own twist of fate led me into the business I own today, shaped by a heart attack at age thirty-four that forced me to reassess my life's direction. This unexpected health crisis became a catalyst for steering not only my career into a new direction, but to change the processes and sales orientation that corporate financial planning had for so long been the accepted way. It was the wake-up call I needed to embrace my passion for empowering others through financial guidance, transcending the conventional boundaries of my industry. This unexpected adversity became a catalyst for embracing the new unconventional path in leadership.

Embrace resilience: Understand that resilience is not just a personal trait; it's a skill that can be cultivated. When faced with challenges, don't view them as roadblocks but as opportunities to develop your resilience and determination.

## EMPATHY AS A GUIDING LIGHT

My own personal struggles alongside client experiences have reinforced the importance of empathy in leadership. I've learned that financial decisions, like life decisions, are often deeply personal and emotionally charged. This realisation has led me to approach leadership with a compassionate heart, forging stronger connections with those I serve. Empathy has become a guiding light, illuminating the path toward more meaningful and impactful leadership.

I have faced as an advisor the worst possible scenario I can think of – the sudden loss of a client. I visited Paul in the hospital the day he died, and his last request was to continue to advise and care for his family. His wife was left not only with the immense grief of that loss but also the daunting task of making crucial financial decisions for the future of her family. Years later, the weight of that grief still burdens her, making it difficult to navigate her financial affairs, the constant memory of why the fund exists. It is in moments like these that I truly understand the profound impact empathy can have. I sit with her, not just as a financial advisor but as someone who genuinely cares about her wellbeing. Together, we work through her financial challenges at her own pace, providing the emotional support she needs. This experience, in particular, reinforced my belief in the power of empathy to transform lives, not just through financial guidance but through the human connection it fosters. Empathy, indeed, remains a guiding light in my leadership journey, reminding me that our roles as leaders extend far beyond the professional realm, touching the very essence of people's lives.

Lead with empathy: Empathy is the bridge that connects you with your team and those you lead. Approach leadership with a compassionate heart, and you'll find that your ability to inspire and influence others grows exponentially.

## EMBRACING THE FLUIDITY OF CHANGE

Life is an ever-evolving journey, and so is the landscape of leadership. My own experiences have taught me to embrace change, adapt to new circumstances and view leadership as a dynamic, evolving process. I encourage those I lead to do the same, fostering a proactive mindset toward growth and development. I've come to believe that there is no such thing as perfect balance in leadership. Instead, there's a perfect imbalance at any one time. This concept acknowledges that life is dynamic, and leadership must adapt accordingly. Just as we can't perfectly balance on a seesaw, we must find equilibrium in the ever-shifting terrain of our professional lives.

I live this concept daily, wearing multiple hats as a business owner, a single mother, a dedicated triathlete and an author. At any given moment, my energy and passion might lean more toward one role than the others. It doesn't diminish the importance of the other aspects of my life; rather, it reflects the reality that true success in any endeavour requires unwavering motivation and commitment. This fluidity allows me to pivot as needed, ensuring that each facet of my life receives the attention it deserves, ultimately contributing to my growth as a leader who embraces change and encourages others to do the same.

Embrace change: Change is the only constant in life and leadership. Instead of resisting it, learn to adapt and thrive in ever-evolving circumstances. Be open to new ideas and approaches, even if they deviate from the conventional.

## THE STRENGTH IN VULNERABILITY AND TRANSPARENCY

Leadership is often seen as a symbol of strength and authority, but I've learned that true strength lies in vulnerability and transparency. Sharing experiences and opening up about our own challenges can create deeper connections and foster an environment of trust and authenticity. As a leader, I've embraced vulnerability and transparency, creating a space where others feel safe to do the same. This has led to more meaningful interactions and a stronger sense of unity within my teams.

Indeed, the act of writing this chapter and sharing personal life stories is a testament to the power of vulnerability and transparency in visionary leadership. By opening up and revealing the challenges I've faced and the lessons I've learned, I hope to inspire others to do the same and create a culture of openness and authenticity within their own leadership journeys. This, I believe, is an integral part of leading by example and fostering growth not only in ourselves but in those we lead.

Embrace vulnerability: Vulnerability is not a weakness but a strength. Share your experiences and challenges openly, creating an environment of trust and authenticity. This will encourage your team to do the same and foster deeper connections.

## ACCEPTING CHALLENGES AS OPPORTUNITIES TO GROW

Life has a way of presenting challenges that, at first glance, seem insurmountable. However, I've come to see these challenges as opportunities for growth. They are the moments when we are pushed beyond our comfort zones and forced to confront our fears and limitations. For me, participating in triathlon training provided a metaphorical journey of facing challenges head-on. It taught me that to succeed, one must embrace fear, confront the unknown and persevere through adversity. These experiences have profoundly shaped my leadership style, emphasising the importance of resilience and courage in the face of challenges.

Challenges are catalysts for growth: Don't shy away from challenges; embrace them as opportunities to learn and grow. It's often in the face of adversity that we discover our true potential.

## A CONTINUAL QUEST TO LEARN

In the decade I spent as an executive financial advisor at two of the top four banks, I learned that leadership is a journey of continuous learning. It's an openness to new knowledge and experiences, both through professional networks and from the diverse individuals and businesses

I've encountered. This willingness to admit that there is always more to learn has been instrumental in my growth as a leader. My approach encompasses personal experience and lessons learned throughout the years, setting me apart from peers and allowing each client interaction to be a unique opportunity for growth.

Embracing this philosophy, I embrace every new client as an opportunity to learn something new. I recognise that no two people or personal situations are the same, yet I also understand that similarities can potentially be drawn upon for the benefit of another client in the future. This perspective keeps me grounded in the reality that I do not know everything, and indeed, no-one does. It's this continual quest to learn and adapt that keeps my leadership fresh and dynamic, ensuring that I can provide the best guidance and support to those I serve.

Commit to lifelong learning: Leadership is a continuous journey of growth and development. Be open to learning from various sources, including your own experiences and the people you encounter.

My own leadership journey has been a testament to the power of embracing the unconventional. It's a journey marked by unexpected challenges, personal growth and a relentless passion for making a meaningful impact on the lives of others. Through trials and triumphs, I've learned valuable lessons that have not only shaped my leadership style but also redefined my approach to financial planning.

Measuring the impact of my leadership is a dual journey. While client success stories serve as my guiding light, I equally rely on introspection and leading with empathy. I assess my own effectiveness by the same metric, considering how my leadership feels, not just to others but within myself. This internal evaluation ensures that my leadership remains authentic, empathetic and consistently focused on making a profound and heartfelt impact on those I serve and lead.

As a visionary leader, I aim to leave a legacy of empowerment and transformation. I want to be remembered for challenging the norm, inspiring others to think unconventionally and showing that leadership is about more than just authority; it's about creating opportunities for growth and change.

## THE PATH FORWARD

The road to success is often riddled with challenges, and giving up can sometimes seem like the easiest option. However, it's during these challenging moments that we have the opportunity to achieve the extraordinary. By holding on, persevering through adversity and embracing change, we can navigate the waves of life and emerge stronger on the other side. As a leader who challenges the norm, I've cultivated a style that blends expertise with innovation. My approach is not just about titles and positions; it's about nurturing resilience, empathy and an unwavering commitment to growth and transformation. Leadership is not a static destination but a dynamic journey where unconventional thinking can lead to remarkable outcomes.

As you embark on your own leadership journey, remember that life's unexpected lessons are some of the most profound teachers you will encounter. Embrace resilience, lead with empathy and view change as an opportunity for growth. Allow vulnerability to be your strength and remember that challenges are catalysts for personal and professional development. Commit to a lifelong journey of learning, drawing wisdom from various sources.

Finally, don't hesitate to challenge the norm and explore the unconventional path; that's often where the most extraordinary leadership stories are written. Unconventional thinking can lead to remarkable outcomes and redefine the boundaries of what is possible in leadership. By infusing these principles into your leadership style, you can chart a course that not only achieves success but also leaves a lasting legacy of positive impact and transformation. Embrace the unconventional and let your leadership journey be a testament to the remarkable heights one can reach when they dare to be different.

# ABOUT AMANDA

Amanda Thompson is an award-winning financial planner, author, ironwoman and the founder and director of Endurance Financial. Whether she's launching her own business, facing a cancer battle or qualifying three times for the Ironman World Championships, Amanda has never been afraid of a challenge.

Endurance Financial is particularly driven to help women overcome the gender biases that stand in the way of personal achievement; lessons learned after thriving in typically male dominated environments. Amanda draws on her twenty years of financial advising and life experiences to educate and mentor in a relaxed and relatable way to support women overcome their fear of finances and own their financial future.

Amanda renews personal and business confidence by providing the financial knowledge and confidence to have a great relationship with money allowing you to become your own CFO (confident, focused and on top of your finances).

As a dynamic keynote speaker Amanda is able to captivate audiences with her intelligent wit and real life stories. She is particularly driven to help men and women overcome the gender biases that stand in the way of personal achievement; lessons learned after thriving in typically male-dominated environments.

# DIAH YUSUF
# NAVIGATING THE WORLD OF
# ENTREPRENEURSHIP & EMPOWERMENT

*Design your own success, winning your life, winning your future.*

MY JOURNEY IN THE world of entrepreneurship and empowerment has been an emotional roller-coaster, marked by triumphs, challenges and an unshakable commitment to driving positive change. As a strategic partnership business advisor, I've had the privilege of founding Indonesia Prima, an organisation dedicated to empowering Indonesian enterprises and aligning them with sustainable development for a better life. In this chapter, I invite you to join me on a deeply personal exploration of the highs and lows, the passion and purpose, that have defined my path.

The inception of Indonesia Prima was a momentous step in my life. It wasn't just about founding an organisation; it was about realising a vision that had been brewing within me for years. I wanted to create a platform that would not only support Indonesian enterprises but also serve as a catalyst for sustainable development. This journey began with a dream, a vision of an Indonesia where businesses thrived and people enjoyed better lives. It was this vision that propelled me forward, even when the road ahead seemed daunting.

The early days of Indonesia Prima were filled with excitement and uncertainty. Building a team, establishing partnerships and defining our mission were no small tasks. However, the support and dedication of like-minded individuals who shared my passion for empowerment made the journey worthwhile. Together, we became a development centre, dedicated to nurturing an entrepreneurial mindset, skill set and spirit.

My work with Indonesia Prima has been an emotional journey in itself. Witnessing the growth and transformation of countless entrepreneurs has been both rewarding and heartwarming. As we explored, maintained and leveraged their innate potential, I saw dreams take shape, businesses flourish and lives change for the better. These moments of empowerment have left an indelible mark on my heart.

Being an entrepreneur myself, I've ventured into various sectors, from health and beauty retail to the dynamic world of property. Each business has been a unique emotional journey, filled with its own set of challenges and victories. The beauty of entrepreneurship lies in its unpredictability; it's a constant dance between risk and reward, and I've embraced it wholeheartedly.

In the property industry, I've learned the art of patience and perseverance. Real estate is not just about transactions; it's about creating spaces where dreams can be lived. It's about understanding the needs of individuals and families and providing them with homes where they can build memories. This emotional connection to the business has been a driving force for me.

One of the most enriching aspects of my journey has been establishing partnerships with business chambers from around the world. These connections have opened doors to new cultures, ideas and opportunities. However, forging international alliances was not without its emotional challenges. It required stepping out of my comfort zone and learning to communicate across cultural divides. The journey taught me the value of empathy and adaptability.

My role as a strategic partner for foreign companies looking to expand into Indonesia and the ASEAN region has also been emotionally fulfilling. It's about bridging gaps, facilitating growth and nurturing relationships. The trust placed in me by these companies and the impact of their investments on local economies have been a source of immense pride and satisfaction.

My dedication to empowering small- and medium-sized enterprises (SME) in Indonesia has been a personal mission close to my heart. Since 2005, I've been actively involved in projects aimed at uplifting SMEs. One of the most emotional chapters of my journey was when one of Indonesia's largest BUMN companies appointed me as project director for Buddy SMEs at PT Telkom Indonesia, Tbk. This role allowed me to directly impact the growth and sustainability of countless SMEs.

Sharing my knowledge and experiences on national and international stages has been an emotional journey of its own. Speaking at events such as the ICSB World Congress, the SME World Forum and the Women Economic Forum has been a privilege. These platforms have allowed me to connect with diverse audiences and share my passion for women in entrepreneurship, SME internationalisation and sustainability. The emotional connection I feel with these causes drives me to continue advocating for positive change.

My leadership roles in global organisations like the International Council for Small Business (ICSB) have broadened my horizons and deepened my commitment to advocating for small businesses and entrepreneurship worldwide. Serving as the secretary-general of the Indonesia Council for Small Business and other positions at the global level have been emotionally fulfilling. It's about being part of a global community dedicated to fostering entrepreneurship and economic growth.

My commitment to women's empowerment has been a cornerstone of my journey. As the chairwoman of Womenpreneurs Indonesia Networks (WIN), working directly with the Ministry of Women Empowerment and Child Protection in the Republic of Indonesia, has been deeply emotional. Witnessing the strength and resilience of women entrepreneurs has been awe-inspiring. It's a reminder that when women are empowered, families, communities and entire nations benefit.

My contributions to global networks have allowed me to collaborate with individuals from diverse backgrounds. Initiatives like One Global Women Empowerment (OGWE) have the potential to create a gender-equal future worldwide. These efforts have not only been intellectually stimulating but emotionally rewarding as well.

Being appointed as the G100 Global Chair for the Business Accelerator Wing has been a humbling experience. Leading one hundred country chairs, including the Denim Club, and collaborating with respected global chairs in other sectors, has been a testament to the power of collective action. G100, a group of one hundred global women leaders, is dedicated to creating a gender-equal future and advocating for women's empowerment worldwide. The emotional connection I feel to this mission is profound.

I actively contribute by writing entrepreneurship articles in national magazines every month. Additionally, I've had the privilege of collaborating on global conferences and reports that aim to inspire and empower women entrepreneurs worldwide. Initiatives like the Women Entrepreneurship Global Conference and Global FIVE (Female Innovative Vision on Entrepreneurship) have allowed me to contribute to the UN 2030 Agenda on Sustainable Development Goals (SDG5). These experiences have been emotionally charged, as they align with my deep-seated belief in the power of entrepreneurship to drive positive change.

Indonesia Prima has forged crucial partnerships for global business advisory, pitching to investors through collaborations like Bzns Builder Egypt and supporting startups through Rainmaking Innovation Taiwan. We've also worked closely with UN Women Indonesia on coaching programs for the Women WeLearn Project. Today, Indonesia Prima is preparing programs for investors interested in partnering with Indonesian SMEs. Our aim is to facilitate curated Indonesian SME businesses that are poised for growth and understand local market dynamics.

As I reflect on my entrepreneurial journey, a kaleidoscope of emotions and experiences rushes through me. From the founding of Indonesia Prima to my involvement in various business ventures and global initiatives, this voyage has been filled with highs and lows, challenges and triumphs. In these concluding moments, I'd like to distil the essence of this journey into five key takeaways for business leaders seeking to make their mark in the ever-evolving world of entrepreneurship and empowerment.

## 1. PASSION FUELS PURPOSE

Throughout my journey, the driving force behind my endeavours has been unwavering passion. It is the spark that ignites the fire of purpose. As business leaders, we must connect with what truly moves us, for it is this passion that fuels our commitment to making a difference. Whether it's building an organisation or launching a venture, infuse it with the essence of your passion, and it will become a beacon guiding you through the darkest of storms.

## 2. ADAPTABILITY IS THE KEY TO SURVIVAL

In the entrepreneurial realm, change is the only constant. My journey has taught me the paramount importance of adaptability. Whether it was navigating diverse business sectors, forming international partnerships or embracing new roles, adaptability has been the compass that kept me on course. Business leaders must be willing to pivot, evolve and embrace change as a source of growth and innovation.

## 3. EMPOWERMENT BEGETS TRANSFORMATION

The heart of my journey lies in the empowerment of others – entrepreneurs, women and SMEs. I've witnessed firsthand the transformative power of empowerment. When individuals are given the tools, knowledge and support they need to thrive, remarkable changes occur. Business leaders should remember that true leadership is not about control; it's about empowering others to reach their full potential.

## 4. COLLABORATIONS FORGE SUCCESS

One of the most valuable lessons from my journey is the significance of collaboration. Partnerships, whether local or international, have been instrumental in achieving goals and driving impact. In the interconnected world of business, collaborations can provide resources, expertise and new perspectives. Business leaders should actively seek out opportunities to collaborate, as it often leads to innovative solutions and expanded horizons.

## 5. A GLOBAL PERSPECTIVE YIELDS GLOBAL IMPACT

My involvement in global initiatives has underscored the importance of thinking beyond borders. In today's interconnected world, business leaders must adopt a global perspective. This means embracing diversity, understanding different cultures and recognising that global challenges require global solutions. By engaging in international networks and initiatives, we can magnify our impact and contribute to a more inclusive and equitable world.

In closing, my entrepreneurial odyssey has been a journey of passion, adaptability, empowerment, collaboration and a global perspective. These key takeaways serve as guideposts for business leaders who aspire to navigate the complex and ever-changing landscape of entrepreneurship.

As you embark on your own journey, remember that it is not only about the destination but also about the profound transformations that occur along the way. Embrace the challenges, celebrate the victories and never lose sight of the positive change you can bring to the world through your leadership and actions.

Your journey, like mine, can become a beacon of hope and empowerment for others, lighting the way for a brighter future.

# ABOUT DIAH

Diah is very enthusiastic to be involved and to dedicate her time through many social communities, and to work on government projects which have helped develop SME in Indonesia since 2005, as well as develop her own business. She founded Indonesia Prima as a strategic business support organization with global network to developing accountable Indonesian enterprises which aligning with sustainable development for better life. The roles as a development centre for exploring, maintaining and leveraging entrepreneurial mindset, skillset and spirit for better life. Indonesia Prima provides continues improvement acceleration for entrepreneurs who are looking for best support for their optimum achievement including preparing connecting with investors. Diah also actively learned and completed several local and international entrepreneurial workshops and certification.

She holds PhD from Rai University India in 2022. The honoris causa doctorate given as appreciation for her dedication for empowering small medium enterprises globally.

She also as business consultant and business advisor for many business owner and organisation in Indonesia and other country. She is certified as business advisor from GrowthWheel International (USA), Transformation Academy (USA) and Cherie Blaire Foundation (UK).

Diah, also as SVP Asia Council for Small Business (Indonesia), Secretary General of Indonesia Council for Small Business (2020 – 2022), Director ICSB Womenpreneurs Indonesia (2021), former vice president for Community Empowerment International Council for Small Business Indonesia (ICSB Indonesia) 2018 – 2020 and as former board member as vice president for Partnership International Council for Small Business Global (ICSB Global) 2018 - 2020. The International Council for Small Business (ICSB) is a non-profit organisation devoted to continuing management education for entrepreneurs and small businesses. Founded in 1955, the International Council for Small Business (ICSB) was the first international membership organisation to promote the growth and development of small businesses worldwide.

She is also chairwoman of Womenpreneurs Indonesia Networks (WIN) inaugurated and advisory directly by Ministry of Women Empowerment and Child Protection Republic of Indonesia, WIN is a platform for strengthening women in entrepreneurship, health and family harmonising. In global organisation, she is also as a vice president of India – Peru Business Council WICCI (Women's Indian Chamber of Commerce & Industry).

Her contribution and strategic thinking on how to empower Indonesia SME, attracting one of the biggest Indonesian BUMN Companies to appoint her as Project Director for Buddy SMEs PT Telkom Indonesia, Tbk and as a vice dean for Wonderful Start-up Academy, Tourism Ministry Program.

As an entrepreneur, she is also leading several businesses in the health & beauty retail area, property industry, smart agriculture, sustainable aquaculture farming, also in social enterprises as the founder and chairman of the Indonesian Entrepreneur Festival, a yearly program for the Indonesia Development Entrepreneurship with the tagline #BersatuMenguat.

She has also been invited many times as a public speaker for both national and international events, mostly discussing women in entrepreneurship, SME internalionalisation and sustainability. She has spoken at the sixty-fourth ICSB World Congress, Egypt 2019 then 1st SME World Forum, Macau 2019 then Urban Campus, Mexico 2019, APEC Financing Opportunities Fair for Women-led MSMEs, Taipei 2019, 65th ICSB World Congress, Paris 2021, World Marketing Forum 2021 and latest in Annual Women Economic Forum, India 2022 and many more.

As Indonesia Presidency G20, she also spoke at officially W20 Forum, March 2022, she brings the topics of financial support for women ultra micro and micro enterprise as part of economic recovery and suggested points to be follow-up. Also, as speaker at the official B20 Side Event: Women in Business Action Council, June 2022, about accelerating the inclusion of women MSMEs in the global economy.

Diah also as part of OGWE (One Global Women Empowerment) launched by B20 G20 Indonesia Presidency 2022, this platform will apply in all G20 countries.

Her contribution in global networks is still broadening as she has been appointed as G100 Global Chair for Business Accelerator Wing. In her wing she will lead 100 Country Chair including Denim Club and connect with respected Global Chair in other sectors. G100 is group of 100 Global Women Leaders with the vision to create an equal, progressive & inclusive environment for women worldwide and an empowered group of 100 women leaders from across the world, leading 100 global wings, supported by 100 He for She champions (Denim Club) and 100 Country Chairs for powerful advocacy, awareness & impact across governments and organisations for a gender equal future.

She actively wrote articles on entrepreneurship in national magazines every month. She also contributed in ICSB MSME Report 2020 issued on UN MSME, 27 June 2020 with thirty-two writers globally. Recently, with five colleagues from Egypt, Australia, USA, Argentina and France, she co-chaired the Women Entrepreneurship Global Conference with ICSB Global (icsbglobal.org/weconference), the conference was successful in inspiring women all over the globe and will continue to develop this activity and spread the impact. Continuing as co-founder of Global FIVE (Female Innovative Vision on Entrepreneurship with colleagues from USA, Argentina, French and Egypt. Global FIVE network works to develop and promote a new approach to female entrepreneurship, joining theory with practice, providing a platform for women to exchange and share all aspects of their entrepreneurial journey thus aiming to address inclusion and equality to further achieve the UN 2030 Agenda on Sustainable Development Goals (SDG5).

Now, Indonesia Prima have partnership with GrowthWheel International for global business advisory, and Bzns Builder Egypt, a business platform to pitch the investor. In the startup community, Indonesia Prima also have a partnership with Rainmaking Innovation Taiwan for support Start-up both country and ASEAN, including match making with VC's in the network. In 2020, Indonesia Prima also have cooperation with UN Women Indonesia to do coaching programs for Women WeLearn Project. Indonesia Prima are currently constructing a program for an investor who will hopefuly be willing to partner with Indonesian SME Business, Indonesia Prima SME Investment Consultant and Accelerator. We provide curated Indonesian SME Business which are already established and having promising growth as well as knowing local market consumption and ready to scale up. Most international businesses and investors know that modern Indonesia boasts a substantial population and a wealth of natural resources. But far fewer understand how rapidly the nation is growing. With this program, it will assist, coaching and monitoring the SME on behalf of the investor for assure their optimum growth.

# DR AISHAH TUL RADZIAH
# THE JOURNEY OF A VISIONARY LEADER

*Be courageous, and stand up for what you believe in. Be sure you have a good story to tell the next generation.*

FROM THE EARLIEST DAYS of my childhood, I exhibited a streak of independence and a firm resolve that would later define my journey as a visionary leader. Growing up with my single mother, we eked out a living by tending to rice paddies and fishing in the river. These humble beginnings instilled in me a strong work ethic and a sense of responsibility that I carry with me to this day.

One of the most influential aspects of my upbringing was my mother's insistence on teaching me the art of cooking. Even before I had reached double digits, I was already preparing meals for the family. Little did I know that this early exposure to the culinary arts would serve as a foundation for my future endeavours. I became adept at whipping up delicious dishes with remarkable speed, a skill that would later become invaluable.

My entrepreneurial spirit also began to emerge during my school years. I took it upon myself to sell cookies and snacks to my classmates, unaware that this youthful venture was nurturing the seeds of entrepreneurship that would blossom in my adult life. However, life threw me a curveball when I contracted chickenpox, sidelining me from school for a gruelling six months. It was a challenging period, but little did I know that this setback would be just a minor detour in the grand trajectory of my life.

As I transitioned from secondary school to the University of Malaya, my academic path took a significant turn. While I had been an art student in my earlier years, I shifted gears to immerse myself in the world of pure science. Physics, biology and chemistry became my companions as I pursued my dream of attending medical school. In 1978, I proudly graduated with an MB;BS Degree (Bachelor of Medicine; Bachelor of Surgery), marking the culmination of my formal education.

Entering the workforce, I faced the challenges of the medical field during my compulsory service in a government hospital. The rigid authoritarianism of some of my colleagues did not sit well with me. It was during this time that I began to envision a different path for myself, one where I could provide health care on my terms, with empathy and a human touch.

In July 1982, I took a leap of faith and established my own clinic and maternity home. Over the years, it thrived under my guidance, becoming a trusted institution for thousands of patients. However, the demands of running a busy clinic took a toll on my health. Neglected lifestyle choices led to obesity and health issues, forcing me to confront the importance of wellness in my own life.

I embarked on a journey to reclaim my health, and it was a transformational experience. Over the course of five months, I shed 19kg, not only regaining my ideal weight but also rekindling my passion for health and wellness. It was this success that ignited my desire to manufacture healthy foods, especially for those battling obesity.

With a wealth of experience and a newfound commitment to health, I founded Dr Aishah Solution Sdn Bhd in May 2010, a manufacturing company focused on innovative, healthy and halal foods. This marked a significant shift in my career, and I was driven by a powerful vision and mission.

My vision was clear: to produce premium, creative and innovative foods that promote a healthy lifestyle. My mission was equally profound: to create premium, creative, innovative, halal and safe healthy foods accessible to people from all walks of life. I aimed to inspire optimism, happiness and rejuvenation through smart and healthy eating while addressing health issues, particularly obesity, through education and professional counselling.

However, the transition from a medical practitioner to a food manufacturer was not without its challenges. Malaysian consumers were not accustomed to the concept of granola cereal and energy bars, which were at the heart of my product lineup. Undeterred, I educated people about the benefits of these products, and it took two years to see positive results. Granola Crunchy, one of my earliest creations, became a hit, and today, it remains one of my bestselling products among the fifteen I offer in Malaysia.

Recognising a societal need and driven by my passion for quality and scientific research, I developed products tailored to combat the obesity epidemic. My goal was to improve the quality of life for consumers of all ages by providing healthier and tastier food and beverage choices. I shared the concept of nutrition as a balanced and enjoyable relationship with food, emphasising health and wellness.

My commitment to innovation and creativity did not waver. Over the years, I earned international recognition and awards for my products, including the Sial Innovation Middle East award in 2014, the Gulfood Award in 2015 and subsequent honours in 2016, 2019 and 2022. Through it all, I remained true to my vision and mission, forging a path as a visionary leader in the world of healthy foods.

Today, I face a new challenge – one that surpasses the hurdles of managing a clinic. While I never had to worry about attracting patients to my clinic, introducing innovative, healthy foods to the Malaysian market has been a different story. But I am undeterred. I have a vision, a mission and a legacy to build, and I know that the journey of a visionary leader is one that continues to evolve and inspire, no matter the obstacles.

## CONCLUSION: REFLECTING ON MY JOURNEY AS A VISIONARY LEADER

As I look back on my life's journey, I find myself humbled and inspired by the path I've travelled – a path marked by resilience, innovation and a relentless commitment to a vision and mission. My story, from a modest childhood to becoming a visionary leader in the realm of healthy foods, offers several key takeaways that resonate not only with my experiences but with the broader principles of leadership and entrepreneurship.

## 1. RESILIENCE IN THE FACE OF ADVERSITY

My life story underscores the first essential lesson – resilience in the face of adversity. From my early days as a young student selling cookies and snacks to my struggle with obesity and health issues, I encountered countless challenges. Yet, I refused to be defined by setbacks. Instead, I used them as opportunities for growth and transformation. This ability to bounce back, surmount obstacles and turn adversity into stepping stones is a hallmark of visionary leaders. It serves as a poignant reminder that setbacks are not roadblocks but rather catalysts for success.

## 2. INNOVATION AND ADAPTABILITY

The second crucial lesson from my journey is the significance of innovation and adaptability. My transition from a medical practitioner to a food manufacturer was a daring move, motivated by a deep desire to enhance the health of my community. Despite initial resistance from the Malaysian market, I persevered, tirelessly educating consumers about the advantages of healthy foods. This chapter of my life emphasises the importance of embracing new ideas, adjusting to evolving circumstances and having the courage to pioneer innovative solutions. My success in introducing granola cereal and energy bars to Malaysians demonstrates that visionary leaders often thrive in uncharted territories.

## 3. VISION AND MISSION AS GUIDING PRINCIPLES

The third and most pivotal lesson from my life's narrative is the power of a clear vision and mission as guiding principles. My vision to produce premium, creative and innovative foods that promote a healthy lifestyle, coupled with my mission to provide halal and safe healthy foods for all, have been the driving forces behind my endeavours. These principles not only informed my actions but also inspired me to educate and uplift my community. Visionary leaders, myself included, are guided by a higher purpose, and our unwavering dedication to our mission propels us forward, even in the face of daunting challenges.

## CONCLUSION

In closing, my life's journey serves as a testament to the transformative potential of resilience, innovation and a commitment to a vision and mission. From my early years of responsibility and hard work to my role as a pioneering force in the realm of healthy foods, my story is a source of inspiration for all.

My hope is that my journey will encourage you to embrace challenges, think innovatively and remain steadfast in your pursuit of meaningful change. As we celebrate the publication of *Able Visionary Leaders,* my story stands as a shining example of the passion of a visionary leader – a story that continues to inspire and empower me.

# ABOUT AISHAH

From childhood and primary school days I had been independent and firm in my stand. My mother who was a single mother drilled me into being a hard and responsible daughter.

We made a living growing rice in the padi fields and catching fish in the river and padi fields too.

Picking up herbs in the nearby forest was a way that enriched my knowledge and helped my to understand the richness of the popular traditional Malay herbs. My mother drilled into me the art of cooking. I cooked foods for lunch before going to school at early tender age of nine. Thanks to her I am now a kind of expert at whipping up tasty foods. I also sold cookies and snacks at school not realising that it was to help nuture my entrepreneuship in later life. I was down with chicken pox for six months until I almost dropped out of school.

I served the compulsory service in the government hospital from the year 1978 to early 1982. I hate the excessive authoritarianism predisposition of the medical registrars and consultants who I worked with.

I established my own clinic and maternity home in July 1982, managing it until 2007. I then down scaled it to a polylinic and maintain it untill now). My health and wellness took a dive in 2003 because of pressure of work resulting in neglected unhealthy lifestyle. I was obese and carried with it the health libilities.

I spent valuable time to start realigning myself onto the right track of health and wellness. I kickstarted the change with a battle cry 'A healthy doctor walks hand in hand with healthy patients.'

It took me five months to pull myself out of the obesity trap with a well planned healy eating habit and healthy lifestyle. Alhamdulillah, I shed off 19kg of my fat fix deposit in five months. I won the battle and regained the ideal weight of 49kg. For the past twenty years I am able to keep a healthy body weight. This success was a factor that triggered my wanting to go into manufacturing healthy foods which can help people who are obese.

Statistics:  1). Deliveries – 25,000
2). Gynaecology – 38,000
3). Minor operations – 40,000

In May 2010 I established Dr Aishah Solution Sdn Bhd, a Woman Majority (share) limited manufacturng company in F&B category. This enabled me to go full swing into manufacturing innovative, healthy and halal foods.

## VISION

My vision is to work smart to be able to be a producer of premium, creative and innovative foods to help people towards a healthy lifestyle.

## MISSION

My mission is to prpduce premium, creative, innovative, halal and safe healthy foods for all walks of life.

We inspire moments of optimism, happiness and a sense of rejuvenation through smart and healthy eating. We are also keen to provide solutions to various health problems especially obesity through education through education and professional counselling.

Our business culture is focused on innovation and creativity.

I now face a different challenge; bigger than the challenge in managing my clinic and maternity home. Previously I did not have to worry getting customers/patients to my clinic. Manufacturing healthy foods, granola cereal and energy/granola bars posed totally different problem. I am very proud of being the first person in Malaysia to venture into this endeavour but alas Malaysians are not ready for this type of food. I was ill informed that granola cereal and energy/granola bars are totally alien to the population.

The show had to go on.

Initially I developed four products with my in house team. I spent some time to educate people to understand granola cereal and granola/energy bars. It took me two years to see the positive result. Consumers accepted my product Granola Crunchy. Now Granola is my most salable product and becomes 'a product hooked'. Presently I have fifteen products commercially in Malaysia.

I recognised a need in society and applied the latest scientific findings to develop suitable products to combat the raging obesity problem. My passion for quality and the use of the latest scientific research help to improve the nutritional value of my products.

I aim to improve the quality of life of consumers at all stages of their existence and offer them healthier and tastier food and beverage choices.

I share the concept of nutrition with consumers, in the sense of a healthy, balanced and joyful relationship with food, together with the logically connected keywords of 'health' and 'wellness'.

I do not rest on laurels but continued to develop new product on a constant basis. I won several international recognations and awards for my products over the years.

I am proud to share with you the following awards which I had won.

The first was in 2014, S.I.A.L. Innovation Award Middle East for my product Energy Bar Durian, Abu Dhabi. Again in 2015, S.I.A.L. Innovation award Shanghai Award for my product Energy Bar Durian.

In 2015, Gulfood Award the Best New Halal Food for my Energy Bar Matcha, in Dubai.

In 2016, S.I.A.L. Innovation Award, Paris for my product Granola Rich.

In 2019, Gulfood Award for New Found Food for Health and Wellness, Dubai.

In 2019, Women CEO Summit & Award, Bangkok December 2019.

In 2020, Gulfood Award the Most Innovative Halal Food for my Protein Granola Sacha Inchi and Protein Granola Spices.

I stay true to my vision and mission.